For more information visit our web site
www.oup.co.uk/general/vsi/

Charles O. Jones

THE AMERICAN PRESIDENCY

A Very Short Introduction

OXFORD
UNIVERSITY PRESS

OXFORD
UNIVERSITY PRESS

Oxford University Press, Inc., publishes works that further
Oxford University's objective of excellence
in research, scholarship, and education.

Oxford   New York
Auckland   Cape Town   Dar es Salaam   Hong Kong   Karachi
Kuala Lumpur   Madrid   Melbourne   Mexico City   Nairobi
New Delhi   Shanghai   Taipei   Toronto

With offices in
Argentina   Austria   Brazil   Chile   Czech Republic   France   Greece
Guatemala   Hungary   Italy   Japan   Poland   Portugal   Singapore
South Korea   Switzerland   Thailand   Turkey   Ukraine   Vietnam

Published by Oxford University Press, Inc.
198 Madison Avenue, New York, NY 10016
www.oup.com

Oxford is a registered trademark of Oxford University Press

Library of Congress Cataloging-in-Publication Data
Jones, Charles O.
The American presidency : a very short introduction /
by Charles O. Jones.
p. cm. Includes bibliographical references and index.
ISBN 978-0-19-530701-6
1. Presidents—United States.
2. Executive power—United States.
I. Title.
JK516.J636 2007
352.230973—dc22
2006031314

5 7 9 8 6
Printed in Great Britain by
Ashford Colour Press Ltd.,
Gosport, Hampshire
on acid-free paper

To Wanda, Elizabeth, Lou, Bob, and Ruth,
from their brother. Somehow we all made it.

Contents

Preface

I am, at this writing, living with my thirteenth president—from Herbert Hoover to George W. Bush. I don't remember much of anything about Hoover, though my midwestern family talked about him rather proudly because he came from Iowa. I have strong personal and scholarly impressions of the rest. I recall the day in 1944 when I came to live in Canton, South Dakota, with my grandparents. I was sporting an FDR button. My grandfather made me take it off. He liked Truman even less, though my grandfather's plainspoken style reminded me of Truman. Put it this way: Had they met, they would have understood each other.

I paid attention to presidents through my school and college years, wondering how you got to be one. Having had FDR as my first impression, and in spite of my grandfather, I thought they were superhuman. Later I learned that it was the expectations that were beyond human. And so I have watched presidents pass through, fascinated by their efforts to manage responsibilities well enough to receive credit for the good as ballast for the certainty of blame for the bad.

The management of disproportionate and often conflicting expectations is the theme of this book. Quite remarkably, the urges that were present in Philadelphia at the writing of the Constitution are still evident today. We want to hold presidents accountable for what happens in government, but we don't want them to have too much power. So we hedge our bets all around by granting powers, then checking, balancing, and sharing them.

It would be fair to hold the system responsible and all those who make it work over time and across issues. After all, presidents are in-and-outers, seldom get all they want, and much of what happens is a result of actions by others (including previous administrations). Trouble is, a system isn't individual or personal, and so it is hard to say who is at fault when things go bad. Yet it is precisely then that we typically want accountability. And so there they are, the presidents as chief executives, the names we all learn. It is their time of accountability—we even mark our political eras with their names: the Roosevelt, Eisenhower, or Clinton years.

I strive in this Very Short Introduction to portray the challenges of presidential leadership in a separated powers system. Executive accountability is a part of that system—it goes with the job. Members of Congress answer to different voting publics; judges respond to the law. It was by no means certain that the system would last, but it has. I have endeavored to explain why and to contribute to understanding how.

Charles O. Jones
Wintergreen, Virginia

Acknowledgments

I am indebted to the many scholars, journalists, and politicians who have, over the years, taught me about the presidency. The list is too long to include here, although a few are cited in notes and references. It is no surprise, however, that Dick Neustadt heads this list. Those familiar with his work will spot its influence in these pages.

Given the purpose of this series, I asked a few nonexpert, politically aware friends and neighbors to react to my original proposal. The comments of David and Georgia Orphan, Bob and Kathy Knowles, Lou and Toni Jones, Reg Hall, and Vera Jones were very helpful, full of common sense suggestions that I followed to the letter. Three anonymous scholarly reviewers also provided useful reactions to the proposal.

Kate Hamill, then at Oxford University Press, worked with me to refine the proposal further, as well as to reassure me that the project was worth doing. Dedi Felman took over as the editor once the chapters were written. She has a remarkable capacity to spot what can be done better and to estimate an author's skill for achieving more. Her editorial nudgings were consistently on target, substantially improving the manuscript.

Others at Oxford University Press were also helpful in overseeing the production of the book. Michele Bové searched for and found appropriate pictures, in addition to managing the transformation of manuscript to book. Helen Mules oversaw the copyediting process and other details; Mary Sutherland improved the text with her careful copy editing; and Peter Brigaitis and Marie Nuchols prepared the index. Each stage was skillfully handled and for that I am most appreciative.

The book is dedicated to my remarkably talented sisters and brothers. I am forever grateful for their love, support, and good humor. Fact is, we are a very funny (all meanings) group in a somewhat less than amusing world.

Illustrations

Tables

Chapter 1
Inventing the Presidency

Imagine being present at the founding of a nation. Who will have powers? How will those with powers be chosen? Will there be one leader or many? How will the government be organized? Will it last? These and other questions faced the Founding Fathers, men like James Madison, Benjamin Franklin, Alexander Hamilton, Gouverneur Morris, Edmund Randolph, Roger Sherman, and George Washington, the most illustrious political thinkers and practitioners of public affairs of the era.

Not willing to repeat the governing errors made by others in those days, the Founders looked for new answers. That quest explains why it would have been so exhilarating to be in attendance, not to mention attending dinner parties with Ben Franklin. The creative work of this group in writing the Constitution of the United States in Philadelphia in the summer of 1787 has been interpreted and invoked regularly in political and policy debate for more than two centuries.

The first founding, a weak confederation ratified in 1781, had failed. Anxious politicians recognized the faults and met to design a more workable government before it was too late. Their gathering was like no other. It produced a unique plan, one applied ultimately to vast regions across a continent. Seldom in history had conditions been so favorable for institutional innovation.

Among the most experimental creations was that of the presidency itself. It was generally understood that more effective leadership was required. But could that goal be achieved while maintaining sufficient checks to prevent tyranny? The ultimate aim was, therefore, to govern, not merely to control, and the solution was the separation of powers. Presidents would live and work within a constitutional construction that divvied up powers in order to promote and preserve unity. Think about it: *separating to unify.* Pondering that aphorism will enhance your admiration for what was accomplished in Philadelphia, not to mention providing a basis for understanding American government and politics.

The word itself, *presidency,* cannot be found in the Constitution. That label was only later affixed to the executive department of the government. There were executives called "presidents" at the time. New Hampshire and Pennsylvania had them, as did South Carolina. Those chairing the Continental Congress and the Constitutional Convention itself were called "presidents," as was the delegate chosen to preside over the Committee of States under the Articles of Confederation (a more descriptive title would have been "His Nonentityness"). But these were not "presidencies" as the term came to be used to designate an institution of executive powers and functions.

Why the title "president"? Why not "governor," the more common title among the states? The answer reveals a basic dilemma facing the Founders. Americans were understandably wary of executive powers as exercised by the king of England. In fact, the first government under the Articles of Confederation had no executive branch as such. Yet it was generally agreed in Philadelphia that one was needed for more effective governance. The title of "governor" was proposed at different times in Philadelphia but, as one historian notes, it "brought to mind the hated royal and proprietary governors of colonial times."[1] The title "president" was more neutral, possibly less commanding, deriving as it does from *praesidere,* essentially "to preside." And that is how the presidents of the Constitutional Convention and the Continental and Confederation Congresses served; they presided.

"President" it would be then, suiting the need for an executive title that was both nonthreatening and uplifting. After experiencing other forms, from English rule to an executiveless Confederation, "Americans needed a positive definition of the role and functions of the executive."[2] A mostly new title for the head of state marked a beginning in that pursuit. The debates over the executive's reach and status in the separated system had, however, just begun. All presidents would ponder their place in the national government precisely because it was never explicitly set forth. Each would have to devise means to comprehend and meet the challenge I posed to you: How to create unity in a separated system.

George Washington: The Founding Presider

If faced with developing a positive impression of executive power, one could hardly wish for more than a George Washington as the first president. He might have been called "George the Reluctant" for the number of times that he had expressed a preference for staying at Mount Vernon over serving in top leadership positions. That reluctance made him even more desirable as one not coveting the job, especially given the disputes among those who did yearn to serve.

There he sat, presiding over the Constitutional Convention, his very presence offering reassurance that each increment of power vested in the president would be judiciously exercised. Pierce Butler, delegate from South Carolina, explained that the president's powers would not "have been so great had not many of the members cast their eyes toward General Washington as President: and shaped their ideas of the Powers to be given to a President, by their opinions of his Virtue."[3] He was the general who defeated the British and then went home. "His Excellency" was not a designation he would invite. And, in fact, when a committee included that title in its report to the Convention on August 6, 1787 a motion was made and passed to have it removed.

The prospect that Washington would be the nation's first president also reinforced the Convention's steady progress toward equality and independence of the branches. Early proposals were weighted toward a prevailing Congress to include having the executive chosen by that body. The weakness of the Articles of Confederation had, however, amply demonstrated the need for an executive with status independent of the legislature, perhaps by separate election. Washington's character and personality facilitated styling the presidency as an office not beholden to Congress, thus contributing to the development of a government of separated powers.

At the Creation

Most people have had experiences in governing, for example, a school board, business group, labor union, charity board, or condo association (very nasty politics that). Therefore, had you been at the Constitutional Convention, it would not surprise you to see committees formed. They serve such critical functions: defusing contentious issues (or discovering they cannot be defused), refining proposals, identifying effects, and integrating ideas. Table 1.1 shows the committees of the Convention, listed in the sequence of their service. The Committee of the Whole acted to get the Convention under way by processing early ideas and plans as delegates were arriving, the Committee on Detail pulled together the agreements reached and proposals pending on vital questions during the first six weeks, the Committee on Postponed Matters faced up to the unresolved and most contentious matters (including that of the presidency), and the Committee on Style prepared the final set of provisions. Had you been there, membership on the Committee on Postponed Matters would have been the preferred assignment. Read on for the reasons why.

Table 1.1 Committees at the Constitutional Convention, 1787

Committee	Purpose
Of the Whole	Essentially presenting the Virginia Plan as the working document (report on June 13)
Of Detail	Assemble provisions agreed upon for further debate (report on August 6)
On Postponed Matters	Resolve outstanding issues for further debate (report on September 4)
On Style	Prepare the penultimate version of the Constitution for review (report on September 12)

Source: Compiled by author.

The most pronounced views at the Constitutional Convention were those of the Anti-Federalists who were mostly content to make corrections to the Articles of Confederation, and the Federalists who wanted a strengthened central government of real authority. The views and recommendations of these two factions were incorporated into two plans offered to the delegates. The New Jersey plan was little more than a revision of the Articles; the Virginia Plan aimed to create a more powerful national government. Neither was as bold as the final document.

Critical to any restructuring was establishing an independently elected executive. And embedded in that issue was whether there would indeed be a separation of powers. Not surprisingly then, forming what would become the presidency was deliberate and deliberative. For as Alexander Hamilton later wrote in *Federalist No. 67*: "There is hardly any part of the system which could have been attended with greater difficulty in the arrangements of it than this [the executive department]; and there is, perhaps, none that has been inveighed against with less candor or more criticized with less judgment."

The evidence for the heated exchanges alluded to by Hamilton can be found in the series of decisions culminating in Article II dealing with the executive. The Convention went back and forth on fundamental issues regarding executive selection and powers. Why? Forming legislatures and courts was familiar work for those several Framers and their friends who had been involved in writing or serving under state constitutions. They were less acquainted with how to create a separate, independent, consequential, yet forbearing executive. Several delegates were fearful of going too far in allocating powers to the executive, understanding that there would be presidents to follow Washington who may not be as reluctant to seek or exploit those powers. In fact, even those Federalists supporting a strong central government originally provided for the executive to be chosen by Congress in the Virginia Plan.

Work on the presidency at the Convention occurred in four phases: (1) testing various ideas in early June, (2) more serious review of issues in mid July, (3) reactions to committee reports in August, and (4) amending and endorsing the final arrangements in early September. Substantively the progression was from an executive selected and constrained by Congress to one independently elected and possessed of significant domestic and foreign policy authority.

The principal issues in the debate over the executive were selection, one executive or more, term length, succession, removal, and powers. All were vital, but the matter of selection determined the separation of powers since a president elected by Congress could not truly be separate from that branch. So that is the place to start.

Selection

It was not until September that the Convention agreed to independently electing the executive. The Virginia and New Jersey plans both proposed having the executive elected by the legislature. The difference was that the Virginia Plan provided for a two-house or bicameral legislature, the New Jersey Plan for a one-house or unicameral legislature.

Selection by a bicameral legislature was included in the report of the Committee of the Whole on June 13, and later in the report of the Committee of Detail on August 6. No particulars on balloting were included in either report. The Committee of Detail report simply stated "His Excellency" [the title proposed for the president] "shall be elected by ballot by the Legislature."

Having the executive elected by the legislature would have resulted in a parliamentary system once political parties were formed. Whichever party, or coalition of parties or factions, was in the majority would likely have selected one of their own to serve as president. The United States would then have been governed by a unitary, not a separated, system. That is, one branch, the legislature, would choose the leader of another, the executive. At the least, the separation of powers requires the separation of executive and legislative elections.

Election by the legislature was approved at first, primarily as a point of departure. Still, the delegates were divided on the issue between those wary of an independent executive (the Anti-Federalists) and those for a strengthened executive (the Federalists). The first group favored legislative election, the second favored popular vote or electors chosen for the purpose of selecting an executive. The matter was so divisive and the subsidiary issues so interwoven (for example, term length and succession) that the final resolution was left to the Committee on Postponed Matters. As it happened, those favoring an independent executive had a majority on the committee, and the Electoral College was born. Popular election of the president never had sufficient support among the delegates and so another system had to be found, essentially a hybrid incorporating legislative and state interests.

The Electoral College system perplexes many Americans and virtually all foreigners. However, it was not designed to confuse (although referring to an institution with neither faculty or students as a "College" is not exactly clear). The proposal was a masterful attempt to suit contending points of view. The legislature would have bearing on the presidential election in two important ways: (1) the number of electors for a state would be equal to the number of representatives allocated to the state on the basis of population plus two for its senators and (2) the House of Representatives, voting as states, not individuals, would choose the president should no one candidate receive a majority of electoral votes. The Senate, voting as individuals, would choose the vice president under those circumstances. Finally, the states would determine how electors would be appointed, including the option of their being popularly elected.

The plan was approved at the Convention by nine states to two (voting being by states, not individual delegates), the same count that had initially favored election by the legislature, a remarkable turnaround in the delegates' thinking. Thus it was that the separation of powers was fixed in the Constitution by dividing the elections of the legislature and the executive. As it has developed in practice, presidential candidates have campaigned nationally to gain a majority of electors, members of the Senate and the House have campaigned in the states and congressional districts. The result is three interdependent national readings of the voting public, one each by the results for president, senators, and representatives.

One or More

The government of the Articles of Confederation provided that "A Committee of the States," with one delegate from each state, be responsible "for managing the general affairs of the united states." One of the delegates was to be appointed "president" to serve no longer than one year in any term of three years. The limitation of this arrangement—a president with severely limited tenure working with an executive committee—was a primary motivation for constitutional change. Therefore, designing more effective management of "general affairs" had to consider whether to have one executive or a committee or council.

Given the failures of the government under the Articles and the weakness of most executive arrangements in the states, it was surprising that any of the delegates supported a plural executive. But the most senior delegate in age, Benjamin Franklin, was an advocate, having supported a twelve-person executive council in his state of Pennsylvania. John Dickinson from Delaware also favored a three-person executive, one each for the northeastern, middle, and southern states. And the New Jersey plan provided for congressional election of a plural executive (number unspecified).

A motion for a single executive was debated very early in the proceedings and passed, seven states to three, on June 4. Thereafter the issue would not be seriously revisited. However the executive was to be elected, however long the term in office, and whatever the eligibility for succession, the executive department would be headed by a single person.

Term Length and Renewal

How long should the single executive serve? Four years now seems obvious, but it came to the delegates quite late in the proceedings. And should the person be term-limited? These were contentious issues at the Convention, as they were allied with the very essence of executive powers in the new government. Hamilton, who wrote most of the *Federalist* essays, explained the advantages of longer terms in *No. 71*: "It is a general principle of human nature, that a man will be interested in whatever he possesses, in proportion to the firmness or precariousness of the tenure by which he holds it; will be less attached to what he holds by a momentary or uncertain title, than to what he enjoys by a durable or certain title;

and, of course, will be willing to risk more for the sake of the one, than for the other." Yet, while durable, an executive elected for a long term bore the features of life-serving monarchs whom most Americans despised. Therefore the longer the term, the more likely it was that the executive would not be eligible to serve again.

There was reluctance on this issue to emulate either the states or the Articles of Confederation. Annual election was typical in both, often including a form of term limitation (for example, having to wait for a period years—the number varied—before serving again). Most delegates agreed that one year of service was too short, but those most fearful of a strong central government, the Anti-Federalists, were also dubious about permitting renewal regardless of the length of the term in office. Why? Because some states with one-year terms and reeligibility had governors reelected over and over again. In New York, with three-year terms, voters reelected George Clinton six times. "Little wonder, then, that so many Americans worried that reeligibility would mean a president for life."[4]

It was not surprising that several proposals for term length and renewal were offered in Philadelphia. Lacking historical practice with different term lengths, one person's estimate as to what would work well was as good as another's. Early in the proceedings it was agreed that the executive should serve a single, seven-year term. Ineligibility for a second term was subsequently removed, then reinserted in late July.

Uncertainty about what was best led to delegates' changing their minds along the way. I picture the debate on this subject as a kind of term-length auction: "I have six years. Do I hear seven? Seven years? Six and a half?" At different times there were proposals for a renewable six years; single eight-, eleven-, fifteen-, and twenty-year terms; for no more than six years' service in twelve; and during good behavior (essentially a life term for the well comported). Many delegates participated in the numbers game.

Given the disparate proposals and uncertain effects, the issues of term length and renewal were sent off to the Committee on Postponed Matters, a convenient and useful means for settling matters not resolvable in full session (are you beginning to understand why I recommended this committee?).

The Committee settled on four years, a shorter term than had heretofore been proposed but with no restrictions on eligibility for second or subsequent terms. The plan was a victory for those favoring a strong executive and, hence, was criticized during the ratification debates in the states as inviting the corruption of electors in the Electoral College by an executive anxious to serve for life.

As it happened in practice, George Washington helped immeasurably to allay these fears. He declined to serve a third term in 1796, thus seemingly introducing a two-term limit, one that was not broken until 1940 when Franklin D. Roosevelt ran for a third, then a fourth, term. In 1951, the Twenty-second Amendment limiting the president to two terms was ratified. Henceforth Washington's precedent would be officially a part of the Constitution.

Removal

In 1998 the American people learned about impeachment. In accordance with procedures set forth in the Constitution, President Bill Clinton was impeached by the House of Representatives, and tried and acquitted by the Senate. The Chief Justice of the United States, William H. Rehnquist, presided over the Senate trial.

Several of those supporting the president in 1998–99 questioned the propriety of the accusers, asserting that they were, in essence, seeking to nullify Clinton's reelection in 1996. It was an argument reminiscent of Alexander Hamilton's summary of the issues involved in impeaching a president as set forth in *Federalist*

No. 65: "A well-constituted court for the trial of impeachments is an object not more to be desired than difficult to be obtained in a government wholly elective." Hamilton predicted correctly that an accusation leading to impeachment and trial would "agitate the passions of the whole community." Therefore, a process for accusing and trying public officials had to be carefully designed. And it was.

Impeachment is a method for defining and enforcing limits on executive and judicial behavior, essentially insuring that no one is above the law. The Founders use of this concept was derivative of English law. "Nowhere did they [the Framers] more evidently take off from that [English] law than in drafting the impeachment provisions."[5] Ultimately, both the substance and process of

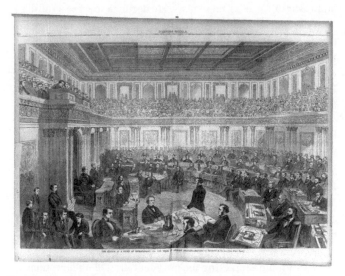

Fig. 1.1. The Senate sits as a court for the removal of an impeached President Andrew Johnson in 1868. As with Clinton in 1999, Johnson was acquitted. (*Impeachment trial of President Andrew Johnson.* Wood engraving after T. R. Davis, *Harper's Weekly* 12 [1868]: 232–33. Library of Congress, Prints and Photographs Division, LC-USZ61-269)

impeachment replicated that of English practice. The terms "Treason, Bribery, or High Crimes and Misdemeanors" (Art. II, Sec. 4) were those used in English law. "Treason," and "Bribery" were obvious enough as deserving of impeachment; "high Crimes and Misdemeanors" were less certain, yet more likely to be used as a basis for bringing charges. Accordingly, intense debate was likely in those rare circumstances when a president was the subject (two occasions only: Andrew Johnson, 1868, and Bill Clinton, 1998, although Richard Nixon was threatened with impeachment, 1974, prior to his resignation).

The functions—sufficient accusation to impeach and try—were divided between the popularly elected House of Representatives, which was given the job of actual impeachment, and the elite-chosen Senate (by state legislatures prior to the ratification of the Seventeenth Amendment in 1913), which was responsible for the trial. This practice also followed the English model of "the role of prosecutor to the [House of] Commons while the [House of] Lords sat in judgment."[6]

But the Framers also were experienced with impeachment provisions in state constitutions. Those states providing for impeachment offered several methods for trials. So the Framers knew of options for managing the problem identified by Hamilton of removing an official who had been elected by the voters.

Reporting on August 6, the Committee of Detail opted for having impeachment tried before the Supreme Court, perhaps emulating the House of Lords, which served judicial functions in England. This proposal was controversial. Who would then try the justices if they were to be impeached? And guess what? The issue was left for the Committee on Postponed Matters. As with the Electoral College, the Committee settled on a masterful compromise. The Senate would try cases, with a two-thirds majority required for removal, and the Chief Justice of the United States would preside. Accordingly, the Supreme Court would play a role, and the super majority would "help the Senate rise above partisanship and deliberate in a relatively dispassionate way."[7] (as was judged to have been the case with Clinton).

The removal provisions were linked in the minds of delegates to those of election, reelection, and length of service. The fears of the Anti-Federalists and others suspicious of a strong national government might have been realized absent a method for impeachment and removal. Including such means suited the checks and balances essential for a system of separated powers.

Allocating and Defining Powers

By definition, executive powers tend to be derivative. An object is required for execution to occur. Laws can't be enforced before they are enacted; standards are not set in the abstract but to effect an agreed-upon purpose. It was, then, perfectly logical for the Founders to work first on delineating the powers of Congress, then to specify: "The executive power shall be vested in a President of the United States of America," and finally to outline the judicial power of the courts in Article III. The sequence—Article I–Congress; Article II–Presidency; Article III–Judiciary—follows the ordinary progression of governance from law making to its implementation and review.

This same point explains why it was unnecessary to specify each and every executive power. It was enough, for example, to state in Article I, Section 8, that "The Congress shall have Power To lay and collect Taxes." That specification implied that the executive would implement what Congress directed to be done, for example, to collect the taxes designed by Congress from those persons or groups specified in the law. Most Americans know just how that works in the case of the income tax, as administered by an executive agency—the Internal Revenue Service.

However, there were executive functions too that had to be defined in the Constitution. Who would make vital appointments? Who would command the military? Who would make treaties and assume other foreign policy functions? What would be the legislative role for the president? Who would act in national or international emergencies? These were among the most important governance-related issues that arguably could have been assigned to Congress as well as the executive. It is useful to be reminded that the answers to these questions are now familiar. But in 1787, each had to be explored, debated, and settled within the context of an overarching principle of the separation of powers.

Appointments

Designating the authority to make appointments was bound to be contentious given the inevitable competition among institutions in a separated powers system. Should Congress have that authority as a check on the executive? Or was that prerogative necessary for an effective executive? And who should be eligible to receive an appointment? In particular, should members of Congress be able to serve simultaneously in the executive or judicial departments?

As noted, the Virginia Plan provided for the legislature to elect the executive, essentially creating a parliamentary or unitary system. It might then have been logical for the plan to allow legislators to serve as ministers in the executive branch (as, for example, with members of Parliament in the United Kingdom). But it did not. Legislators were not only "ineligible to any office established by a particular State, or under the authority of the United States," but, as well, they were not eligible for a period after leaving Congress.

The "ineligibility" provision was debated extensively, with a consensus developing on not permitting simultaneous service but serious questions raised about denying appointments for a period after departing. As finally resolved, ineligibility during legislative service was approved, and there was no provision added to disallow legislators having left Congress from being appointed, as many have.

The issue of who makes appointments was critical to the creation of a separation of powers system. The status of each branch was at stake. The Virginia Plan proposed that the legislature create tribunals and appoint judges. This provision was refined early in the Convention by giving the Senate the authority to appoint judges. The August 6 report of the Committee of Detail distributed appointments as follows: the treasurer would be appointed by the Legislature; ambassadors and judges of the Supreme Court by the Senate, and "officers in all cases not otherwise provided for by the Constitution" by the president.

As it had on other issues, the Committee on Postponed Matters chose a more executive-oriented process, one not previously voted on in the Convention. The president was given the authority to nominate, "and with the advice and consent of the Senate," appoint "ambassadors, and other public Ministers, Judges of the Supreme Court, and all other Officers of the U[nited] S[tates], whose appointments are not otherwise herein provided for." The recommended language was almost exactly that finally adopted. The president was also given authority to fill vacancies during the recess of the Senate, and Congress could by law invest appointment of inferior officers "to the President alone, in the Courts of Law, or the Heads of Departments" (Art. II, Sec. 2). In the end, the Committee on Postponed Matters once again favored a distribution of powers such as to maintain a balance among the three branches. How might you have voted on this issue?

Military

Among the president's greatest powers was one to which the Constitutional Convention devoted relatively few words: "The President shall be Commander in Chief of the Army and Navy." Seemingly it was assumed that the executive would manage the militia, as was the case in the states. The more critical issue, of course, was that of deciding which branch would commit the nation to war.

However momentous the decision to declare war, it received relatively little attention in Philadelphia. As accepted as it was that the president should command the militia, so was it generally acknowledged that Congress should have the power to declare war. The only question was whether it should be the prerogative of the Senate only, and whether Congress had the power "to make war" or "to declare war." Making war suggested management and command. The report of the Committee of Detail used the words "make war," but on a floor motion the words were changed to "declare war." As one delegate pointed out, making war might be understood as "conducting" war, which properly would be an executive function.

Treaty Making

Lacking an executive, foreign policy and treaty making had to be managed by the unitary legislature under the Articles of Confederation. It was inevitable, then, that the Convention would have to decide how to allocate these matters if they were to agree on a separated powers system. It was likewise predictable that strengthening the executive, as happened during the course of the proceedings, would include an enhanced role for the president in foreign policy. After all, there was no single leader of a bicameral legislature. Even still, it was not until the final weeks of the Convention that treaty making was shifted from the Senate to the president.

Not unexpectedly, your Committee on Postponed Matters once again strengthened the president's role by reporting the following language: "The President by and with the advice and consent of the Senate, shall have power to make treaties. . . . But no Treaty shall be made without the consent of two-thirds of the members present." As reported in James Madison's notes, the debate focused on three issues: adding the House of Representatives for its advice and consent, excepting "treaties of peace" from the two-thirds requirement, and allowing treaties by consent of majority vote in the Senate. The first and third amendments were rejected, the second was first accepted, then rejected upon reconsideration. And so the Constitution in final form acknowledged the president as head of state with the authority to make treaties with the advice and two-thirds consent of the Senate.

In practice, this authority conveyed to the president the initiative in foreign relations and international status as leader of the nation. Yet it also counseled foreign leaders that major decisions in the United States government ordinarily involved two or more branches of government. Many provisions in the Constitution may be viewed as tutorials in how a separated powers system works (*separating to unify*). The treaty-making provision was one such.

Legislative Role

Providing a legislative or law-making role for the president was the subject of considerable debate at the Convention. Much of the discussion focused on the authority of the president to veto legislation passed by the House and Senate. Debate focused on what form it should take and what it should take for Congress to override a veto. A related issue was whether to have the judiciary involved in vetoing. The Virginia Plan proposed a "council of revision" composed of the executive and the judiciary to review legislation and issue a "negative" or veto. The proposal was offered on three occasions in Philadelphia but was rejected each time. How would you have voted on that—essentially reviewing the constitutionality of laws as passed rather than awaiting a case before the court?

The idea of the veto itself was widely accepted. Those favoring domination of the executive, like Alexander Hamilton, wanted an absolute veto, that is, no further legislative recourse. This position was soundly defeated. Hamilton was not having a good convention! The issue then was the margin required to override the president's veto, the effect of which would be to enact legislation into law over the objections of the president. The Committee of Detail set the margin at two-thirds of the full membership of each house in its August 6 report. A motion was approved to increase the margin to three-fourths only to be changed back to two-thirds during the final days of the Convention. The two-thirds majority has proven to be a significant hurdle. Only a very small proportion of vetoed measures become law due to overrides.

Less controversial law-making powers were, in time, to become vitally important in strengthening the legislative role of the president. Three interrelated clauses in particular are vital.

— "He may require the Opinion, in writing, of the principal Officers in each of the executive Departments, upon any Subject relating to the Duties of their respective Offices." (Art. II, Sec. 2)
— "He shall from time to time give to the Congress Information of the State of the Union . . ." (Art. II, Sec. 3)
— "[He shall] recommend to their Consideration such Measures as he shall judge necessary and expedient." (Art. II, Sec. 3)

These three provide the constitutional authority for an activist president to designate the agenda for Congress. The first invites the president to draw upon the "Officers" of the departments in framing proposals. The third authorizes shaping this information and proposals into recommendations to Congress. And the second provides a formal giving of information on the State of the Union to Congress. And that is how it has worked in practice as "time to time" has come to be an annual stock-taking and agenda-setting message from the president to Congress. Indeed, with the coming of television, the message is one of those "national moments" that projects where we are as a people, as expressed by the president, his supporters, and his critics in Congress and the media.

Finally, the president is charged with taking "Care that the Laws be faithfully executed." (Art. II, Sec. 3) This was "catchall" language that was introduced in the report of the Committee of Detail on August 6 and carried through to the final report of the Committee of Style on September 12. It was, perhaps, the best that could be done in defining the intentions of executive powers but remains vague as to precise meaning or application. Still presidents rely on this provision to validate an action that, arguably, cannot be justified by expressed authority in the Constitution or by existing statutes. Any such use of this provision by presidents has, through history, been controversial. For that which lacks precise meaning is open to varying, and often partisan, interpretations when applied to issues of major importance.

Conclusion

Inventors are problem solvers. Typically they tinker until they believe they have a workable device. It is often the case that inventors don't know in advance how well or how long their creations will work. The Founders were serious stylists as they worked at creating an executive branch. In so doing, they formed a government of separated powers. They had theories to guide them in their quest but very little practice with this form on a national scale. What they produced was, in the words of Richard E. Neustadt, "a government of separated institutions *sharing* powers."[8] As described above, the executive's role emerged as follows:

The executive progressed from weakness to strength in its shares of powers and competitive status in the government. The earliest decisions would have produced a congressional government, with the executive chosen by Congress and denied certain critical powers of appointment and treaty making. The later decisions provided an executive branch that could hold its own against the other branches, without necessarily being able regularly to trump its competitors.

A strengthened executive contributed to fashioning a separated rather than unitary system of government. Governing powers in the Articles of Confederation were concentrated in the Congress. Creating an executive with shares of governing powers and one independently elected produced a new and untried form of government—the separation of powers.

Table 1.2 Presidential Powers—Congressional Sharing
(Required by U.S. Constitution)

Presidential Powers	Congressional Sharing
Veto power (Art. I, Sec. 7)	Override by 2/3 of both houses (Art. I, Sec. 7)
Election (Art. II, Sec. 1; 12th Amdt.)	Set the time; House chooses president, Senate chooses vice president if no majority in Electoral College (Art. II, Sec. 1; 12th Amdt.)
Commander in chief (Art. II, Sec. 2)	"To declare War . . . To raise and support Armies . . . To provide and maintain a Navy" and other powers (Art. I, Sec. 8)
Make treaties (Art. II, Sec. 2)	Advice and 2/3 consent of Senate (Art. II, Sec. 2)
Selected appointments (including ambassadors, public ministers, and judges of the Supreme Court (Art. II, Sec. 2)	Advice and consent of Senate; vest appointment of inferior officers in others (Art. II, Sec. 2)
Give Congress information on the State of the Union and recommend measures (Art. II, Sec. 3)	"To make all Laws" (Art. I, Sec. 7) "No money . . . drawn . . . but in Consequence of Appropriations made in Law" (Art. I, Sec. 9)
Nominate a vice president in case of a vacancy (25th Amdt.)	Majority vote in both houses (25th Amdt.)
Removal (Art. II, Sec. 4)	House sole power of impeachment; Senate sole power of trying impeachments (Art. I, Secs. 2, 3)

Source: Compiled by author.

Separated institutions sharing powers work within the constraints implicit in their having to share. As any sibling knows, it may be polite, even sociable, to share but it does leave less for you. Sharing can provoke competition so as to get as big a portion as possible. The Founders were ever sensitive to this tendency and worked to provide constraints, often literally forcing cross-institutional consultation and cooperation (see table 1.2). Therefore, even a strengthened executive was constrained by checks and balances.

Effective governance in a separated system requires each branch to be attentive to the others. This principle appeared to dominate the thinking of the Founders. As applied to the presidency, it offers a rationale for the theme of this book: Presidents are not and cannot be as powerful as most people think. What was invented was an executive much stronger than any then existing in America, but one whose strength and effectiveness could only be realized in concert with the other branches. That is the essence of *separating to unify*. At no point in the creation was there any substantial opinion that in inventing the presidency the Founders were establishing *presidential government*. They wanted effective government, one in which the president would lead by being attentive to the legitimate roles played by the other branches.

Creating and strengthening the presidency insured the emergence of a separation of powers. But doing so did not move the United States from a congressional to a presidential system. The lesson is clear: Studying the presidency requires attention to its place in the government of separated institutions sharing and competing for powers.

Notes

1. Forrest McDonald, *The American Presidency* (Lawrence, KS: University Press of Kansas, 1994), 157.
2. Donald L. Robinson, *"To the Best of My Ability": The Presidency and the Constitution* (New York: W. W. Norton, 1987), 19.

3. Quoted in Richard J. Ellis, ed., *Founding the American Presidency* (Lanham, MD: Rowman and Littlefield, 1999), 9.
4. Ibid., 98.
5. Raoul Berger, *Impeachment: The Constitutional Problems* (Cambridge, MA: Harvard University Press, 1973), 54.
6. Ibid, 54.
7. Ellis, *Founding the American Presidency,* 237.
8. Richard E. Neustadt, *Presidential Power: The Politics of Leadership* (New York: John Wiley, 1960), 33, emphasis his.

References

Berger, Raoul. *Impeachment: The Constitutional Problems.* Cambridge, MA: Harvard University Press, 1973.

Commager, Henry Steele, ed. *Documents of American History.* New York: Appleton-Century-Crofts, 1949.

Corwin, Edward S. *The President: Office and Powers, 1787–1957.* New York: New York University Press, 1957.

Ellis, Richard J., ed. *Founding the American Presidency.* Lanham, MD: Rowman and Littlefield, 1999.

Hamilton, Alexander, John Jay, and James Madison. *The Federalist.* New York: Modern Library, 1937.

Kelly, Alfred H., and Winfred A. Harbison. *The American Constitution: Its Origins and Development.* Vol. 1. New York: W. W. Norton, 1948.

McDonald, Forrest. *The American Presidency: An Intellectual History.* Lawrence: University Press of Kansas, 1994.

Neustadt, Richard E. *Presidential Power: The Politics of Leadership.* New York: John Wiley, 1960.

Riker, William H. *The Art of Political Manipulation.* New Haven, CT: Yale University Press, 1986.

Robinson, Donald R. *"To the Best of My Ability": The Presidency and the Constitution.* New York: W. W. Norton, 1987.

Siemers, David J. *Ratifying the Republic: Antifederalists and Federalists in Constitutional Time.* Stanford, CA: Stanford University Press, 2002.

Tansill, Charles C., ed. *Documents Illustrative of the Formation of the Union of the American States.* Washington, DC: Government Printing Office, 1927.

Chapter 2
The Presidency Finds Its Place

Placing the presidency in the new government required answers to two questions of physical location: What city would serve as the capital? Where would the president live and work? Additionally, there was a question of enduring political interest: How would this recently invented executive work with the other branches?

As it happened, the same separationist rationale that evolved in the deliberations of the Constitutional Convention appeared to inform the responses to all three questions. The capital city would be sited in a central location, virtually at a midpoint between the North and South. Congress and the presidency would be located in the city at some distance from each other, with a swamp separating the two buildings. And, save for failing to get a majority in the Electoral College, presidential candidates did not have to go through Congress to win. They were to be independently elected, if interdependently empowered.

Today's visitors to Washington, DC, may find it difficult to believe but there was no such city when George Washington was inaugurated as the first president. Washington took the oath of office on April 30, 1789, on the balcony of Federal Hall, located at the corner of Wall Street and Broad Street in New York City. New York, however, would not remain the executive's launching point for long.

An early debate sought to establish a permanent seat of government. Several locations were proposed as members of Congress favored their own states or regions. As finally resolved in July 1790, a Residency Act set the site for the capital on the Potomac River and authorized President Washington to appoint commissioners to designate its exact location. Meanwhile the government would stay in New York City until December 1790, then move to Philadelphia until 1800, after which a new, centrally located Federal City was expected to serve as the nation's capital.

With the first question of placement answered, the next uncertainties were the capital's precise location on the Potomac River and the design of the city. Land had been ceded by Maryland on the northeast side of the river, and by Virginia on the southwest side (unused, this section was later reclaimed by Virginia). President Washington selected the site, across the river from Alexandria, Virginia, not far from Mount Vernon. He then appointed Major Pierre Charles L'Enfant, a French-born

Fig. 2.1. Major L'Enfant's design for the "Federal City," soon to be named for George Washington. (Library of Congress, Prints and Photographs Division, Historic American Buildings Survey, National Park Service, DC668)

engineer who had served in the Continental Army, to plan a Federal City.

L'Enfant's design was not followed in every aspect, and Washington fired the temperamental planner along the way (*enfant* is French for "child"), but most people today would be able to identify L'Enfant's initial layout with its wide avenues, open blocks of space, and diagonals over an orderly grid as that of Washington, DC. Just as there was a desire at the Constitutional Convention to avoid centralizing power, the Federal City had no central location for government. "L'Enfant's plan physically separated the powers and thus, intentionally or not, gave a geographic expression to a political concept."[1]

There were three governing centers in the new capital: one each for the Congress, the presidency, and the courts at Judiciary Square (though the Supreme Court was never located there). The executive and legislative branches were at the greatest distance (just over a mile apart), with the courts in between. This separation was likely to foster distinct communities, a development that occurred early and continued with the expansion of the congressional and executive workforces.[2] In fact, the distance between the branches allowed the communities to grow without impinging on one another, a condition that changed once the swamp was drained.

What was originally called the "President's House" was designed as both residence and workplace. Also known as the "executive mansion," it came to be referred to as the White House in the James Madison and James Monroe presidencies. How it got that name is a matter of some dispute.[3] The most persuasive explanation is that it was rebuilt and painted white after being seriously damaged by a fire during the 1812 War.

So the answers to the first and second questions regarding real estate were that the presidency would be in a new city designated

26

as the capital and housed at some distance from Congress. In 1790 the city was named for the first president, a decision made by the three commissioners Washington had appointed to assist him in deciding on the site for the new capital on the Potomac. Interestingly, Washington never lived in the city with his name. He is the only president never to have lived in the White House, most assuredly to his relief as John Adams, its first resident president, found it drafty, damp, and lacking a bathroom.

The answer to the third question regarding the place of the presidency in the government depended initially on the framework set in Article II on the executive branch. Three perspectives were evident at the Constitutional Convention in regard to the executive: (1) a *presidential presidency* in which the executive would be the dominant branch; (2) a *congressional presidency* with the executive selected by and thus dependent on Congress; and (3) a *separated presidency* in which the executive and legislative branches shared and competed for powers.

Alexander Hamilton was the principal advocate of a presidential presidency. He proposed that the executive, to be called "Governor," be elected by electors "during good behavior," essentially a life term. The governor would have an absolute veto, full power as commander in chief, unrestricted appointing power for major departments, and the power to make treaties with the "advice and approbation" of the Senate.

There would have been little doubt about who was in charge had this plan been approved. As it happened, there is no need to consider it further. Hamilton's plan received little or no support at the Convention and therefore did not represent an enduring perspective. The only carryover was in the person of Hamilton, who was appointed secretary of the treasury in the Washington presidency, serving for more than five years and consistently supporting a strengthened executive.

The same cannot be said for the congressional and separated presidency perspectives. The first had strong support at the Constitutional Convention among Anti-Federalists, ever wary of a powerful executive and a dominant central government. Indeed, congressional primacy characterized the set of proposals offered to the delegates by the Committee of Detail on August 6, 1787. Congress would choose the executive and have some executive-type functions (for example, treaty-making by the Senate).

Most proposals along these lines were amended in the direction of a more independent executive, one not as strong as Hamilton's but with greater separation from Congress. Yet it was a certainty that those fearful of a too-strong executive would be ever watchful of how presidents interpreted and applied their authority. In fact, the balance of congressional versus presidential powers has been a focus of debate from 1787 to the present (for example, in 2006 in regard to government surveillance of communications by suspected terrorists during the George W. Bush presidency).

The final version of executive powers was that of the separated presidency, one independently elected and with shares of powers separate from those given to Congress. It was the most experimental of the three models and, therefore, the most subject to interpretation over time. Major events and personalities would likely influence the development of a presidency for which there was no analog, as would the need for the executive to work in concert with the other branches. Therein lay the boldness of the experiment, that is, in separating the institutions enough to prevent tyranny but not so much as to produce deadlock.

A Congressional Presidency?

What might have been? Table 2.1 shows the Committee of Detail's recommendations to the Constitutional Convention in regard to

Table 2.1 The Congressional Presidency That Might Have Been: Provisions Relating to the Executive in the Report of the Committee of Detail

Provision	Comment
Elected by the legislature	Seemingly the dominant view until the report of the Committee of Postponed Matters
Title to be "His Excellency"	Almost confirming the executive as ceremonial
7-year term	Many proposals, but 7-year term had the most support (was in the Virginia Plan)
Ineligible for a second term	A longer term justified ineligibility for reelection
Senate given power to make treaties and to appoint ambassadors and judges of the Supreme Court	Ordinarily thought of as executive powers; would have resulted in a weak executive
Legislature to appoint the treasurer	Another executive function given to the legislature
Members of Congress not eligible to serve in any other office; Senators not eligible for one year after leaving office	Having the legislature elect the executive suggests a parliamentary system; making legislators ineligible to serve with the president interfered with development
Legislature given power "to make war"	Suggested that Congress would conduct war, not the commander in chief; later changed to "declare war"
Supreme Court to try impeachments	Changed later to the Senate when questions arose about trying judges

Source: Compiled from the report of the Committee of Detail as printed in Charles C. Tansill, *Documents Illustrative of the Union of the American States* (Government Printing Office, 1937), 171–82.

the executive branch on August 6, 1787. The proposals were in line with the original charter of the Convention, that is, to modify, not discard, the Articles of Confederation. Several proposals were also similar to those included in the Virginia Plan that served as the point of departure for the delegates.

A congressional presidency would have been created by the plan offered on August 6. There would not have been a separation of powers. Congress selected the president and the treasurer; the Senate appointed ambassadors and judges of the Supreme Court. "His Excellency," the president, could serve but one seven-year term. The Senate-appointed Supreme Court would try impeachments. And Congress was given the power "to make war"; the Senate "to make treaties."

Oddly, however, the report included a provision prohibiting members of Congress from serving in executive positions, with senators even banned from such jobs for a year after leaving the Senate. This proposal was at variance with parliamentary systems in which ministers are typically appointed from parliament. The delegates favoring this limitation were anxious to avoid cabals in which members of Congress would divide up the spoils. But the arrangement permitted presidents to select their friends and acquaintances for positions that would, over time, come to have significant powers without clear accountability to Congress.

As set forth in the Committee of Detail, Congress would circumscribe the president's place in the government. Once political parties developed and matured, their members in the legislature would select presidents and attempt to influence their appointments. Presidents would, in turn, be answerable to their party or a coalition of parties, much as in the United Kingdom. Presidents would not have an independent basis of support among voters apart from their public identity with the party. Even then, they would be limited to one seven-year term.

The Founders would have created a congressional presidency, marginally strengthening the executive provided for in the confederation but failing to invent an executive of sufficient independence to qualify as having met the criteria of a separated-powers government. Still this early plan revealed the hesitancy among many prominent delegates about having a strong, independent executive. Therefore, the first presidents were on notice to proceed cautiously in defining their status and exercising their powers.

A Separated Presidency

Through August 1787 and into September of that year, the Convention moved bit by bit toward an executive much less dependent on Congress. Creating an independently elected president with weighty powers over the executive branch was, perhaps, the most striking feature of the new government. However, as is shown in table 2.2, the executive was not strengthened to the point of full self-determination, as Hamilton preferred. The veto could be overridden, treaties made required a two-thirds affirmative vote in the Senate, major appointments were with the advice and consent of the Senate, and the president as commander in chief needed support in Congress to go to war and to support and maintain the military.

The checks listed in table 2.2 were real enough, but their purpose was not merely negative. The Founders were fashioning a mutually dependent law-making system. Each part of the system would support and enable the other two parts. The checks encouraged consultation both ways. In some cases, as with treaties and appointments, the Constitution even called for "advice" from the Senate. But politically savvy presidents would understand the need for communicating with those on Capitol Hill. If they wanted the legislation that they inspired to be drafted and passed, they would need supporters from across the swamp on Capitol Hill. Likewise, if members of Congress wanted their causes

Table 2.2 The Separated Presidency: Powers and Checks (Constitutional Provisions)

Powers	Checks in Congress
Veto bills	Reconsider and pass by 2/3 majorities in both houses
Fail to sign a bill	Becomes law within 10 days (Sundays excepted)
Fail to sign and Congress adjourns	No recourse
Commander in chief	To declare war, raise and support armies, provide and maintain a navy, regulate the land and naval force, call forth the militia, organize, arm, and discipline the militia
Require opinion of cabinet	No provision
Grant reprieves and pardons	No recourse
Make treaties	Advice and consent of 2/3 of senators present
Nominate and appoint ambassadors, other public ministers and consuls, and judges of the Supreme Court	Advice and consent of the Senate
Receive ambassadors	No provision
Fill vacancies during recess of Senate	No recourse
Give State of the Union message	No provision
Recommend measures to Congress	No provision (but require their approval to become law)
Convene both houses or either; adjourn them in case of disagreement	No recourse

(continued)

Table 2.2 (*continued*)

Powers	Checks in Congress
Faithfully execute the laws	No provision
Nominate a vice president in case of a vacancy (25th Amdt.)	Majority vote in both houses

Source: Compiled by author from provisions in the Constitution of the United States.

supported by the president, they would need to be in his favor in order to avoid a veto. Political parties would facilitate this contact. Meanwhile, both the president and Congress would have to be ever wary of court judgments regarding the constitutionality of agreements reached.

Whether and how this concoction of shares of powers would work was uncertain upon the launching of the revised government in 1789. Much would depend on events for testing the capacity of the interlocking system to manage. The sparseness of Article II on the executive provided few clues as to the president's role. Too much was left unwritten or unspecified. A great deal was left to be worked out over time.

Thus, for example, it would have been difficult at first to predict that obligations of the president to give Congress information on the State of the Union and to recommend measures for their consideration would serve vital agenda-setting functions. Nor would it have been apparent that the executive establishment would expand to immense proportions, thus challenging the management capabilities of the president and the oversight capacity of Congress. What may have been foreseen was the variability in style, skill, adaptability, and savvy of individual presidents to fit themselves suitably into the job. And it was apparent that the distributions of powers and the ambiguities in defining these powers meant that presidents would have to orient and reorient themselves to the power grids in Washington

Fig. 2.2. Delivering the State of the Union message—a feature of the separated presidency. (LBJ Library photo by Cecil Stoughton [3-6-WH64])

and outside. That the grids would eventually include thousands of private interests with lobbyists, a huge media component, non-governmental "think tanks," and representatives of foreign governments and international organizations was not at all obvious at the start.

The Perpetual Ordeal

If the Constitution and the government it created were to last, then it was inevitable that there would be two governing populations: those who came and went, and those who stayed on. Elected politicians and their aides mostly constitute the first group, a generalization modified in recent decades with high incumbency return on Capitol Hill. Judges with life appointments and bureaucrats mostly comprise the second group. The first group would grow modestly as states were added; the second, especially the bureaucrats and professional staffs, would grow exponentially. Such developments are in the nature of a maturing government performing its functions in society.

Typically the expectations back home are that elected officials are in charge of the national government. The perpetual ordeal for those coming into Washington and returning home again is to learn enough about the ways of those staying on to direct and administer their work. The ordeal is especially apparent for presidents because more is expected of them, and they are among the shortest of short-termers.

Washington's precedent of serving just two terms lasted for 152 years, finally broken when Franklin D. Roosevelt ran for a third term in 1940 and won. During that span of time, nine of thirty-two presidents (counting Roosevelt) served a full eight years. One of these, Grover Cleveland, won two nonconsecutive terms (winning in 1884, losing in 1888, and winning again in 1892). Two others, Lincoln and McKinley, were elected twice but were assassinated.

Since the ratification in 1951 of the Twenty-second Amendment limiting a president to two terms, three of eleven presidents have served two full terms (Eisenhower, Reagan, and Clinton), with one in his second term at this writing (Bush 43). One other, Nixon, was elected twice but resigned prior to his likely impeachment.

What this record shows is that twelve of forty-three presidents (28 percent) have served eight years (with one pending and one, FDR, having served twelve years). Eight years of service is equal to one and one-third Senate terms or four House terms. Yet most presidents do not serve that long. The average length of service of post–World War II presidents (excluding Bush 43) is 5.6 years— *not even one full Senate term.*

Presidents enter a permanent government for which they will be held responsible. The task was demanding enough at the start. It has come to be colossal with the expansion in the size and reach of the federal government. The challenge is especially daunting for someone who has not had direct governmental experience in Washington, a phenomenon that has occurred even in the modern period (four of the most recent five presidents having come from out of town).

The trial for George Washington as the first president was unique. "When Washington took the oath of office on April 30, 1789, he entered upon an office the nature of which was described only by certain sentences in an untried Constitution." It was not foreordained that he would succeed. But in the judgment of one of the foremost students of public administration, "he was . . . one of the ablest executives ever to hold the office of president."[4] Given the importance of his first appointments, Washington "took meticulous care in choosing the new corps of public officials."[5] Two future presidents served with Washington, John Adams as vice president and Thomas Jefferson as secretary of state. Alexander Hamilton served as secretary of the treasury. Edmund Randolph, a major figure at the Constitutional Convention, was attorney general. It was a strong start in giving life to "certain sentences in an untried Constitution."

Who served first was important because the presidency needed the legitimate definition that Washington and Adams were likely to provide. Jefferson had a different view, one much less supportive of a strong national government and influential executive. From Jefferson's presidency forward into the twentieth century, individual presidents would vary in regard to their perceptions of the role of presidential leadership. Typically events like economic recessions, foreign wars, and, most notably, the Civil War were influential in determining which presidents would be the most active. These events helped to define presidential leadership and explained the high ratings given by historians to Andrew Jackson, Abraham Lincoln, Theodore and Franklin Roosevelt, Woodrow Wilson, Harry Truman, and Ronald Reagan, in addition to Washington.

It was not until the twentieth century that presidents received much help in getting placed in an expanding government. They made appointments but had little personal professional assistance in the White House. This changed dramatically in the post–World War II period. Presidents now have several hundred assistants in the White House Office and hundreds more in a number of agencies in the Executive Office of the President (see chapter 5). These many aides and supporting units serve as liaison to the scores of executive, legislative, and judicial agencies, essentially the president's fingers into the government.

Fitting In

Taking on a new job typically requires more than reading the job description and being sensitive to the growth of the organization. There are more subtle considerations, notably the status of the position at the time of employment. What were the effects of decisions made by the person leaving the job? Were people pleased with the predecessor's performance? What are the expectations in regard to decisions and behavior? One eminent scholar adds this question for presidents: "How do presidents go about the task of fashioning their places in history, and how amenable are these places to being fashioned according to presidential design?"[6]

The true nature and complexities of the job should be thought about before seeking it. In fact, one of the most important questions to be answered in deciding to run is: Why do I want to be president? Answers to the questions mentioned earlier should help with this vital query. Having won, a president's attention naturally turns to styling arrangements that will suit the purposes in seeking the job. But the slate is not wiped clean following an election. An organization already exists. And purposes are being served by policies set in place by previous administrations and congresses. Government is enduring, leadership changes.

Illustrations of the challenges facing new presidents abound. Consider what it must have been like for Franklin Roosevelt to take over in the midst of the Great Depression. Awesome challenges faced him and the Congress. In that case, government organization was insufficient to cope with economic and social issues. New agencies had to be created to administer bold, new policies. Several entering presidents have had wars or their aftermaths to manage—Truman, World War II; Eisenhower, Korean War; Nixon, Vietnam War; the forty-fourth president following George W. Bush, the war on terrorism. Whatever else these presidents wanted to accomplish would have to be designed alongside decisions regarding the wars they inherited.

Other presidents are inaugurated in periods of huge expansions in government services. Eisenhower, a president with a mostly military career, was responsible for managing the New Deal and Fair Deal social programs of Roosevelt and Truman. Nixon inherited the Great Society domestic programs of Lyndon Johnson, a collection of entitlements like Medicare, Medicaid, federal aid to education, and food stamps, which Nixon mostly did not favor, at least in those forms.

The state of the economy and federal debt also can influence a president's options upon moving into the White House. Reagan's priorities were dictated by double-digit inflation, unemployment, and interest rates at the end of the Carter presidency. His tax cuts stimulated the economy, but he mostly failed in an effort to cut back spending. Therefore, he passed on deficits and public debt that would restrict the choices of his successors. Clinton had to act first on the economy due to a recession in 1991–92, having to delay other priorities.

Scandal, too, has had carryover effects for new presidents. Truman (cronyism), Nixon (Watergate), Reagan (Iran-Contra), and Clinton (fund raising and Lewinsky), each affected the presidency and how the next occupant judged it necessary to act, mostly with promises to develop and enforce codes of ethics.

Finally, reforms are often instituted in one presidency to affect another. This topic will be the subject of chapter 7. Suffice to note at this point that once in place, reforms (for example, the War Powers Act or the Congressional Budget and Impoundment Control Act) are seldom then abandoned by subsequent presidents or congresses, even if they are ineffective. Rather they become a part of the institution and therefore must be incorporated into how a presidency is managed.

Passing Through

Think of it this way. Presidents are passing through a history they did not make but can influence. What came before is theirs to manage, along with the events that occur during their tenure and while acting on their own agenda of issues. Judging how to fit in will likely be prompted by how a person comes to be president. Some, like FDR, Johnson, and Reagan, won by huge margins that reflected public anxiety for change. Each of these presidents was expected to propose large-scale programmatic change. They were encouraged to be *assertive* in the early months of taking over the presidency. Taken together, their presidencies were among the most productive of major policy change in recent history—Roosevelt and Johnson being more expansionist of government, Reagan being more consolidative and contractive.

More often, new presidents are advised to be *cautious* leaders because it is difficult to read the public mood. They will have won by the barest majority or, perhaps, by a plurality, making it very difficult to interpret a policy message from the election results. Fitting in requires attention to weaknesses as much as to strengths. Winning by an average popular vote percentage of 47 percent, Kennedy, Nixon, Carter, Clinton, and Bush 43 all had to heed this advice. Some did not. Carter (proposing a sweeping energy program), Clinton (setting national health care as a priority), and Bush 43 (campaigning for major change in Social Security in his second term) pressed forward with limited political or public support to endorse large change, all with limited or no success.

Certain presidents are *custodial* in that they assume office upon the death of their predecessor. Fitting in for Truman and Johnson included sensitivity to the legacy of two popular presidents, FDR and JFK. An argument can be made as well to include Bush 41 as a custodian of the Reagan presidency. He was said by some to be serving Reagan's third term. In each case, the takeover president had to respect the legacy while attempting to fashion a presidency suited to his own preferences—no simple task. Truman and Johnson were successful enough to be elected in their own right; Bush 41 was not.

In other cases, presidents are expected to be *restorative* of the institution because of scandal in the previous administration. Eisenhower, Ford, Carter, and Bush 43 were faced with emphasizing ethics as a priority because of scandals with previous administrations (see earlier discussion). Of these, Ford had the greatest challenge given the scope of Watergate and the resignation of President Nixon. Among other limitations was his having been appointed, not elected, as vice president, his pardoning of Nixon soon after being sworn in, and large increases in Democratic congressional majorities in 1974. His experience gave new meaning to the "perpetual ordeal."

Conclusion

Presidents face the formidable task of judging how to serve. Expectations of their performance vary but are mostly high. At first, presidents had to exercise caution in interpreting their authority. If they had been too aggressive, reforms would likely have been enacted to limit their powers. Through history, presidents have had to adapt to the larger responsibilities associated with a growing population, land mass, and bureaucracy. How each president adjusts to change inevitably affects the nature of the job for the successor. Accordingly, constitutional authority, how those prerogatives are interpreted and put into practice, events and their impacts on governing and government, and the performance, even personal behavior, of one's predecessor combine to delineate the job description for and public acceptance of presidents.

As will be discussed in chapter 3, not all presidents are created equal in the advantages available to them in finding their place in the government. Some come to Washington with little experience in the national government. Others become president by circumstance, the death or, in one case so far, the resignation of the president with whom they are serving as vice president. Presidents in each of these cases have special issues in finding their places.

Notes

1. Gerhard Casper, *Separating Power: Essays on the Founding Period* (Cambridge, MA: Harvard University Press, 1997), 102.
2. See ibid., ch. 4. The development was less clear for the courts. The Supreme Court was located in the Capitol Building until 1935, when it moved into the building on Capitol Hill that it occupies today.
3. As reported in Gilson Willets, *Inside History of the White House* (New York: The Christian Herald, 1908), 39–40.
4. Leonard D. White, "Public Administration Under the Federalists," *Boston University Law Review* 34 (June, 1944): 145.

5. Ibid., 182.
6. Stephen Skowronek, *The Politics Presidents Make: Leadership from John Adams to George Bush* (New Haven, CT: Yale University Press, 1993), 18.

References

Casper, Gerhard. *Separating Power: Essays on the Founding Period.* Cambridge, MA: Harvard University Press, 1997.

Jones, Charles O. *The Presidency in a Separated System.* 2nd ed. Washington, DC: The Brookings Press, 2005.

King, Gary, and Lyn Ragsdale. *The Elusive Executive: Discovering Statistical Patterns in the Presidency.* Washington, DC: Congressional Quarterly Press, 1988.

Skowronek, Stephen. *The Politics Presidents Make: Leadership from John Adams to George Bush.* Cambridge, MA: Harvard University Press, 1993.

White, Leonard D. *The Federalists: A Study of Administrative History.* New York: The Macmillan Company, 1948.

Young, James Sterling. *The Washington Community: 1800–1828.* New York: Columbia University Press, 1966.

Chapter 3

Electing Presidents
(and Other Ways to Occupy the Oval Office)

To invent is to do something differently. The Founders invented a new form of validating executive leadership. Their design not only set forth an untried election system but it also helped shape the opportunities and establish the boundaries of presidential power. Much would be expected of those bearing the title of "President," but their elections provided very different political capital for meeting these demands. And some, one-fourth of those in the twentieth century, were not elected to the office when first entering.

Would it work? No one knew for certain at the start and, in fact, apart from accepting that George Washington would be the first president, no one knew exactly what would happen next. What a story it is! The mystery of the workings of the Electoral College, shared by many today, may have played a role in its preservation. Setting reformist fervor aside, one has to admire the brilliance of fashioning an interlocking system so uninviting to quick fix alterations. Tinkering with one part—term lengths, choice of electors, counting electoral votes, substituting popular election—is fraught with unanticipated consequences.

Try it. Pick a favorite change in how presidents are elected. Then conduct a realistic test of the effects of your change. Think comprehensively about the system. This chapter may assist in that analysis. Mostly what follows will show that constitutional construction and history are on the side of maintaining the unique method designed by the Founders.

The political astuteness of the original formulation did not prevent anomalies in elections following the virtual coronation of George Washington for two terms. Corrections rather than reforms had to be made. For example, in 1796, the first election following Washington's retirement, John Adams and Thomas Jefferson were understandable choices, Adams then serving as vice president; Jefferson for his national stature as the principal author of the Declaration of Independence and the first secretary of state. Adams won narrowly. Having placed second, Jefferson then served with Adams as his vice president. In a contemporary context, it would be akin to Al Gore, then John Kerry, serving as George W. Bush's vice presidents following the 2000 and 2004 elections.

These same two candidates—Adams and Jefferson—ran in 1800, this time with the endorsements of congressional caucuses—Federalists for Adams, Democratic-Republicans for Jefferson. The result as described subsequently was a tie, not between Jefferson and Adams but between Jefferson and his running mate, Aaron Burr. That anomaly had to be corrected and was in the Twelfth Amendment.

The Constitution provided that presidential electors would be appointed by a method determined by the state legislatures. The number of electors allocated to a state was set at the number of representatives plus the two senators. The electors were to meet in each state and vote for two persons. Their tallies were then sent to the president of the Senate to be counted. The person receiving a majority of the votes would be president. Originally, if two persons received an equal majority (as with Jefferson and Burr in 1800), the House of Representatives would choose, with each state having one vote. If no one person received a majority of electors, the House of Representatives would choose among the top five vote-getters. In either case, the person receiving the second most electors would serve as vice president, with the Senate making the choice if two or more had an equal number of votes.

This method of election was unusual by any measure. It disregarded the probability that political parties would develop. It allowed for the popular election of electors but did not require it. Thus an aristocratic method of appointing electors was allowed, along with a democratic method of popular election. And the election of the vice president was a party-less matter—essentially whoever came in second, as with Jefferson serving as Adams's vice president.

How would the system get under way? In the first election in 1789 electors all voted for Washington. How they were appointed made no difference as there was no opponent. Still, the method varied among the states. Some legislatures, in joint session or concurrently, appointed electors; others provided for a variation of popular election and designation by the state legislature. Three states did not participate in 1789: New York because the two houses of the state legislature could not agree on a method, North Carolina and Rhode Island because they had not as yet ratified the Constitution. Washington received sixty-nine electoral votes. Electors had two votes, and while there was no stated opposition to Washington, opinions varied regarding a second choice. John Adams had the most second-ballot votes.

The matter of first and second place was bound to cause problems at some point. What if two persons received an equal number of votes? The Constitution provided that the contest would then go to the House of Representatives. But if that were to happen frequently, as some Founders thought it would, the principle of the separation of powers might be subverted with Congress effectively making the choice. Further, as with Jefferson serving as vice president for Adams, one's opponent might then take over upon the death or resignation of the president.

It did not take long for these issues to be dealt with. In 1800 the then Vice President Thomas Jefferson was a candidate for president. Aaron Burr was, presumably, running for vice president. Both received seventy-three electoral votes. The Constitution specified that electors "vote by Ballot for two persons," making no provision for separate balloting of president and vice president. Under these circumstances, the House of Representatives was directed to "chuse by Ballot one of them for President." (Art. II, Sec. 1) As president of the Senate, Jefferson announced the result: a tie.

As provided in Article II, voting in the House was by states with each state having one vote regardless of the number of representatives. On the first ballot, Jefferson won eight states, Burr six, and the delegations from two states were divided and thus had no vote. Nine states were required for election. It took thirty-six ballots and a great deal of political dealing for Jefferson to get the ninth state.

In 1803 Congress passed a constitutional amendment requiring electors "to vote by ballot for President and Vice President," thereby separating the two positions. The amendment was quickly ratified as the Twelfth Amendment and was therefore in place for the 1804 election. The Electoral College method of selection has not been the subject of other constitutional amendments. The nominating and election processes have, however, evolved over time as quite different from those early contests.

An Evolving System

The ambiguity illustrated by the 1800 election was but one of several issues to be resolved. Who would be the candidates? Would there be political parties? Would presidential and vice presidential candidates run as a team? How would electors be chosen? Answers to these questions illustrate the complexities in proposing reforms. The system came to be interconnected, with political parties taking a strong interest in candidate selection given their stake in team victories.

Events leading to the creation of a United States of America were bound to produce likely candidates for president. The case of George Washington has already been discussed. But there was an ample supply of notable figures actively involved in public affairs: John Adams, Thomas Jefferson, Alexander Hamilton, Aaron Burr, Thomas Pinckney, John Jay, James Madison, and George Clinton, to name a few. Benjamin Franklin too was an eminent figure, though elderly at the founding, and he died a year after. Too bad. A Franklin presidency would have enlivened government, politics, and social life. Consult any biography of the Philadelphian to understand why.

Congressional Caucuses

Congressional caucuses, that is, meetings of like-minded senators and representatives, developed as the means for nominating presidential candidates for several early elections. Their emergence was viewed by some as jeopardizing the separation of institutions that had been achieved at the Constitutional Convention. For if presidents had first to be nominated by members of Congress, would they not then be in their debt? As it was, however, the caucuses during this period, 1804–24, mostly selected expected, if not always certain, choices. Twice, 1812 and 1820, the Democrat-Republicans nominated the incumbent presidents, Madison and Monroe. The Federalists during this time were declining steadily and were no longer a factor by 1820.

The period between 1824 and 1832 proved to be critical for presidential nominations and the development of political parties. In 1824 the congressional caucus system became an issue. A small group of Democrat-Republicans caucused to nominate Secretary of the Treasury William Crawford for president. Other regional candidates did not accept this choice and were nominated within their states. As a consequence the voters and electors were given four choices: Andrew Jackson, Tennessee; John Quincy Adams, Massachusetts; William Crawford, the rump caucus nominee from Georgia; and Henry Clay, Kentucky.

Jackson won a plurality of the popular and electoral vote but did not have a majority of either. Therefore the choice fell to the House of Representatives, again voting by states but this time among the top three, Jackson, Adams, and Crawford, as provided by the Twelfth Amendment. Having run fourth, Clay threw his support to Adams, who won the required majority of thirteen states on the first ballot. Jackson was understandably enraged. President Adams rewarded Clay by appointing him secretary of state. It is interesting that two of the most controversial elections in history, 1824 and 2000, involved the sons of former presidents: John Quincy Adams and George W. Bush.

National Conventions

The brief era of the congressional caucus as a nominating body was over. The circumstances of its demise suggested that a more popular method for selecting presidential candidates had to come into being. It had been made clear in 1824 that the public did not support having members of Congress control who would be their choices for president. The 1824 election also marked the end of the Founders' generation, and with it, the Federalists as a political force. Additionally, the failure of the Democrat-Republicans to unify behind one candidate caused their downfall.

In 1828 Andrew Jackson was renominated by the Tennessee legislature and became the consensus candidate of the new Democratic Party. Those supporting the reelection of President John Quincy Adams called themselves the National Republicans.

There was no disputing the results in 1828; Jackson won the Electoral College by a margin of more than two to one.

Some form of mass party meeting was predictable if the presidential nomination was to come from outside Washington, DC. The first such conclave was held in September 1831 by the Anti-Masons, a third party. The National Republicans followed with a convention in December 1831, also preparing the first party platform, and the Democrats held their first meeting in May 1832. This new form for nominations had staying power, if variable functions, over time. Every major party candidate from 1831 to the present has been formally nominated by a national convention.

It was also predictable that attention would eventually turn to the selection of delegates to the nominating conventions. Those wishing to have influence with or to be rewarded by a president sought first to control state delegations. As political parties gained strength, state and local bosses bargained for appointments and policy with candidate organizations.

On occasions the negotiations carried through to the conventions, with disputes on the seating of delegations, writing of the platform, and choice of candidates. Prior to the development of presidential primaries, multiple ballots were often required to nominate presidential and vice presidential candidates, especially in the Democratic Party because of a two-thirds rule for winning the nomination. Thirteen of the twenty-four Democratic conventions from 1832 to 1924 required more than one ballot. Seven took more than ten ballots, four more than forty (the record was 103 in 1924). The two-thirds rule was abandoned in 1936, and there has been just one multi-ballot Democratic convention since (in 1952).

Republican rules have always provided for a simple majority in nominating their candidates. They had eight multi-ballot conventions of the seventeen between the founding of the party in 1856 and 1920. Just one of these exceeded ten ballots, thirty-six were required in 1880. Subsequently, Republicans have made their nominations with one ballot in all but two conventions, 1940 and 1948. Having lost the drama of choosing the candidate, conventions are of less interest to the public while retaining other purposes, notably for unifying the party in kicking off the general election campaign.

Presidential Primaries

The development and refinement of presidential primaries are major reasons for the one-ballot convention in the modern period. In 1901 Florida was the first state to provide a primary election for choosing delegates to the national convention. Wisconsin followed in 1905, Pennsylvania in 1906, and Oregon in 1910. A dozen states had adopted some form of the primary (either for the selection of delegates or for permitting voters to express preferences among candidates, or both) by the 1912 conventions, another eight by 1916. Enthusiasm for primaries began to wane in the 1920s and '30s. Several states repealed their laws. Most party leaders were not keen about primaries given that they were substituting voter choice for local and state leader control of delegations. During the 1930s public attention was focused on the depression and World War II, with President Roosevelt dominating politics. There were twenty primaries in 1920, just fourteen in 1940, almost none of which was seriously contested in either party.

Presidential primaries were revived following World War II as a popular route to the nomination. Those candidates not favored by party leaders could win if they were able to garner sufficient delegate support. The greater ease of travel and communication enabled prospective candidates to manage national campaigns and potentially to establish front-runner status prior to the convention.

Primaries were important in both the Democratic and Republican nomination battles in 1952. Senator Estes Kefauver (Tennessee) challenged Democratic party leaders by running in primaries. He won twelve of the fifteen in 1952 and forced a three-ballot convention (won by Illinois Governor Adlai Stevenson who had received less than 2 percent of the primary vote). In the Republican Party, General Dwight D. Eisenhower successfully challenged the establishment candidacy of Senator Robert A. Taft (Ohio). Eisenhower won five of the nine contests in which he was entered.

From that time forward, candidates were expected to run and establish front-runner status in the primaries even though a majority of delegates were selected by other means (mostly state party caucuses). The number of primaries increased only slightly between 1952 and 1964 (varying between fifteen and nineteen). But in each case the candidate with the most primary votes won the nomination.

The 1968 Democratic nomination proved to be vital in solidifying the role of primaries. President Lyndon Johnson decided not to seek reelection, thus providing an open race for the nomination. The principal candidates were Senators Eugene McCarthy (Minnesota) and Robert Kennedy (New York). McCarthy won the early primaries before Kennedy entered the race. Kennedy won the critical California primary but was assassinated on the very evening of his victory. Vice President Hubert Humphrey did not enter the primaries, receiving write-in votes only. The principal issue was the Vietnam War, with McCarthy and Kennedy opposed and Humphrey representing the Johnson administration's record.

The convention was among the most tumultuous in history. Humphrey was the choice of party leaders, but he had not been tested in the primaries. Kennedy, the emerging popular choice, was dead. Antiwar activists were desperate. Riots broke out in Chicago, the convention city, as Humphrey won the nomination. Postconvention reform commissions concentrated on insuring a more open process with greater representation of all groups.

These changes encouraged many more states to adopt presidential primaries. The number of primary states increased from the mid-twenties in 1976 to the mid-thirties in the 1980s, the high thirties in the 1990s, and more than forty at the millennium.

By the end of the century, nominations were settled in presidential primaries. The front-runner in each party was selected in every case, 1972–2004. Conventions became ratifying agencies of a choice already made. Additionally, states began front-loading their primaries; that is, moving them earlier in the calendar. Consequently, the campaign for the nomination started earlier, front-runners emerged from the first primaries, and the general election campaign began months sooner than in the past. Understandably, these developments have added to the cost of running for president and have encouraged demands for campaign finance reform.

"Primary campaigning proved to be a perfect match for the visual medium of television."[1] Dramatic developments in communication had a profound effect on the nominating process. Like horse races, campaigns are interesting to follow. They take place in the open, the stakes are high, and they have a finish line—election day. But television, the Internet, and other forms of communication are also incorporated into individual campaigns, at an increasingly high cost in dollars and organizational effort.

The nomination of presidential candidates has evolved historically in several stages: (1) expected choice of national figures; (2) congressional caucus endorsement; (3) national party conventions; (4) conventions supplemented by primaries; (5) primaries establishing front-runners; and (6) primaries determining the choice. These stages reflect intentions to have the public involved, basically responding to more general democratizing developments, such as the emergence of political parties, expansion of suffrage, state electoral reforms, and growth of mass media.

Political Parties: Winning Elections

In *Federalist No. 10*, James Madison warned against "the mischiefs of faction," stressing the need to control their effects. Madison defined faction as "a majority or minority of the whole, who are united or actuated by some common impulse of passion, or of interest, adverse to the rights of other citizens, or to the permanent and aggregate interests of the community." He believed that the Founders had discovered the formula for regulating faction: representative government extended over "a greater variety of parties and interests." Put simply: Make a republic and extend its sphere.

In *Federalist No. 51*, Madison justified the separation of powers and checks and balances by a similar acknowledgment of the need for controls. "Ambition must be made to counteract ambition. . . . A dependence on the people is, no doubt, the primary control on the government; but experience has taught mankind the necessity of auxiliary precautions." Thus it was that the Founders made it virtually impossible for a faction, whether as a political party or interest group, to direct the whole government.

The constitutional design did not, however, prohibit either faction or party. Madison explained that removing the causes of common impulses or interests would be wrong or impractical. A free society thrives on the right to organize in support of common interests. And so it was a matter of *when* and *how* political parties would develop, not *whether*. Table 3.1 shows the major political parties that emerged, as evidenced by winning the presidency. As shown, from 1856 to the present the competition has primarily been the Democrats versus the Republicans. Minor parties have been a factor along the way, but none has achieved lasting national competitive status after 1856.

How have political parties developed? And what difference has it made for the president? It is relevant in responding to these

Table 3.1 Major Political Parties in Competition for Presidency, 1789–2008

Period	Political Party A	Political Party B
1789–96	Federalist	—
1800–16	Federalist	Democratic-Republican
1820–24	Independent Democratic-Republican	Democratic-Republican
1828–32	National Republican	Democratic-Republican
1836–52	Whig	Democrat
1856–2008	Republican	Democrat

Source: Compiled by author from Harold W. Stanley and Richard G. Niemi, *Vital Statistics on American Politics*, 3rd ed. (Washington, DC: Congressional Quarterly Press, 1992), 111–15.

questions to state that Madison and his colleagues designed controls that worked. Federalism, separation of powers, separation of elections, checks and balances, bicameralism, variable term lengths, and the Electoral College have determined how political parties function. The design did not prevent parties or factions from emerging, but it created the world in which they would do their work.

This constitutional structure has nurtured political parties as loose, election-based, mostly nonideological, interest-facilitating organizations of a self-identifying membership. Third parties with more programmatic and ideological orientations have not prospered for long. True, the Republican Party tends to be more conservative, less likely to promote government solutions, and representative of business interests. The Democratic Party tends to be more liberal, more likely to favor a larger role for government, and representative of labor's interests. But both tents are large, and regional differences have been substantial.

It has been said that banks are robbed because that's where the money is. Likewise, political parties organize where the elections are. And by constitutional intention and allowance, elections are everywhere. Most relevant for presidents are those contests for their job and those for the House of Representatives and Senate. In many respects these are all *state* elections, subject as they are to regulations at that level. Accordingly, political parties adjust to state laws that regulate how they organize, select candidates, manage elections, and raise and spend money.

Term lengths have an effect on how political parties organize and function. If presidents, representatives, and senators all had coterminous four-year terms, the political party could conceivably coordinate the campaign messages and fashion leadership strategies for governing. But a president is elected with representatives who are then up for reelection in two years and with just a third of the senators whose terms will not end for six years, two years beyond that of presidents unless they are reelected.

The Founders enforced the separation of powers by separating the elections. In sharp contrast with a parliamentary system, American political parties organize to win the three institutions: House, Senate, and presidency. Each party has campaign committees in the House and Senate to raise money and coordinate election activities. Presidential candidates have their own campaign committees, and the national party committees attempt to harmonize among these units. This separation within the party structure is shaped by the differences among the three types of national elections (president, House, Senate). The campaigns for each vary in fundraising, agenda, the stakes (different term lengths), applicable laws, types of candidates, and connections to state and local parties. The problem of coordinating all of these organizations is avoided by not having anyone in charge!

One clear and wholly constitutional effect of separating national elections is to allow both political parties to win. For example, in 1996 President Clinton, a Democrat, was handily reelected president and Republicans kept their House and Senate majorities. Such split-party results make it difficult to declare a mandate. Seemingly, voters often accept the advice of baseball's Yogi Berra: "When you come to the fork in the road, take it!"

There are six possibilities for split results with two parties and three elections, as shown in table 3.2. All six variations have been realized from the founding of the current two-party system in 1856. Split-party results were common in the second half of the nineteenth century, occurring nearly 50 percent of the time. It was rare during the first half of the twentieth century to have one party in the White House, the other a majority in Congress. In the post–World War II era, however, split-party government has been the common form. Eight of the eleven presidents in that time have at some point faced opposite party majorities in one or both houses of Congress. Remarkably, the parties split control of the presidency and Congress in one twelve-year period, 1981–93, and for 75 percent of the time, 1969–2009.

The consequences for political parties of separating elections and partitioning of terms are profound. The party a president defeated in winning office may command House and/or Senate majorities. In that case, presidents must seek cross-party support in enacting a program. Presidents with opposition party congresses also find that too much compromising with the other side loses votes in their own party. Sometimes you can't even win by winning.

Presidents obviously prefer that their party have majority status in the House and Senate. That advantage, however, does not guarantee loyalty. The partitioning of terms (two, four, and six years) means that all representatives and one-third of senators will face election in two years. The strong incentive on Capitol Hill

Table 3.2 Forms of Split-Party Arrangements, 1856–2009 (with examples)

Presidency	House	Senate	Examples
Democrat	Republican	Republican	Cleveland, 1895–97; Wilson, 1919–21; Truman, 1947–49; Clinton, 1995–2001 = 12 yrs.
Democrat	Republican	Democrat	Buchanan, 1859–61 = 2 yrs.
Democrat	Democrat	Republican	Cleveland, 1885–89 = 4 yrs.
Republican	Democrat	Democrat	Hayes, 1879–81; Eisenhower, 1955–61; Nixon-Ford, 1969–77; Reagan, 1987–89; Bush 41, 1989–93 ; Bush 43, 2007–09 = 24 yrs.
Republican	Republican	Democrat	Garfield, 1881–83; Bush 43, 2001–03 = 4 yrs.
Republican	Democrat	Republican	Grant, 1875–77; Hayes, 1877–79; Arthur, 1883–85; Harrison, 1891–93; Taft, 1911–13; Hoover, 1931–33; Reagan, 1981–87 = 18 yrs.

Source: Compiled by the author from data in Norman J. Ornstein et al., *Vital Statistics on Congress, 2001-2002* (Washington, DC: AEI Press, 2002), 56–58.

is to bring constituency-oriented perspectives to presidential requests. State and local interests often trump party loyalty.

Continuous Testing

Presidential and congressional elections occur by the calendar, not by crises, votes of confidence, or even deaths. Thus, it is entirely possible to have an election with relatively few issues; that in 1988 was said to be one such. By law, presidential and congressional elections occur on the first Tuesday after the first Monday in November. Having a day certain structures the campaign, in terms of organization, candidate activity, and expenditure of funds. Other important dates on the calendar are those for presidential primaries, the two national conventions, and candidate debates.

Polls are taken continuously, often dominating media coverage of the campaign. In the period after World War II, there was but one polling organization—the Gallup Poll. Today there are several. Most major media outlets—national newspapers and magazines, network and cable television—sponsor polls, with state and local polls arranged by media at those levels. Universities and institutes also conduct surveys and polls. And candidate organizations and political parties conduct their own polls.

These measures of opinion are mostly directed at the candidates. Who is ahead and by how much? Tests are taken on issues as well and may influence the campaign rhetoric and debate. Election day ordinarily settles who will be president. An exception was the 2000 election when a recount in Florida delayed the final outcome until mid-December. Until recently, campaigning ceased on election day, and the first stages of governing by a new team began. The political consultants moved on to other clients, and the pollsters conducted fewer tests. All of that has changed dramatically.

Permanent campaigning is now a notable feature of governing. Polls are regularly taken on major issues, and the president's job approval is tested frequently. In his first three years in office, President George W. Bush had a total of 630 ratings of his job performance; 210 a year, nearly 18 a month. Bush 43 was evaluated as many times in a week as President Truman was in a year.[2]

What explains this exponential growth in testing the public's view of the president's job performance? Improvement in the

technology of polling is part of the answer. Now it is easier than in the past to produce, analyze, and report poll results. Why are the results of interest? After all, the president is in office for a fixed, four-year term. Split-party government, a more public policy process, and, more recently, narrow-margin politics help to explain why more polls are taken and why we follow the results. Each cause merits comment.

Presidents having to work with an opposite party majority on Capitol Hill generate interest in their political status in both parties. High job-approval ratings are thought to be evidence of public support, at least at the time of the poll, and are therefore a potential advantage for the president. Members of Congress, especially those from states or districts won by the president, are understandably attentive to these scores.

Related to this development is a tendency for policy debates to be more in the public domain. Virtually all major legislation is now the subject of advertising on television, heated discussion on talk radio and cable news stations, analysis by Internet bloggers, and sometimes mass demonstrations. Hence there are *policy* horse races just as there are *candidate* horse races. It is thought that one way to judge who is winning is to take polls.

Narrow-margin politics have advanced these developments. The 2004 presidential election was the first since 1988 in which the winner garnered a majority of the popular vote, and that by just 51 percent. House and Senate majorities have been thin for a dozen years (1995–2007), thus placing a premium on party unity. Again, the president's political status as measured by public support is a factor in effective leadership of a narrowly divided Congress.

These trends in polling, policy, and politics, encourage presidents to campaign actively and constantly. Contemporary presidents "go public," as the phrase has it.[3] It is now common for presidents to

Fig. 3.1. The Clinton presidency excelled in campaigning for election and for policy. (© visionsofamerica.com / Joseph Sohm)

take to the road following the announcement of a major proposal. In some cases, as with President George W. Bush's proposed Social Security reform in 2005, a full-fledged campaign is undertaken. To conclude, modern presidents are evaluated constantly, and they see it as part of their job to influence those ratings so as to maintain political status.

Who Wins?

The winners in presidential contests are listed in the appendix. The discussion here will concentrate on the period subsequent to the formation of the modern two-party system in 1856. Table 3.3 displays a few basic points regarding who wins. There have been thirty-eight elections and twenty-five elected presidents, 1856–2004 (not counting Andrew Johnson, Chester Arthur, and Gerald Ford, who served but were never elected as president). Republicans have won 61 percent of the thirty-eight elections in the period. Democrats dominated the presidency during just one period, 1932–52, when Franklin D. Roosevelt won four times and

Truman once. Republicans won 74 percent of the elections, 1856–1928 and 64 percent of those, 1952–2004.

Just three Democrats (Wilson, FDR, and Clinton) were reelected from 1856 to 2004 (FDR three times), although Cleveland served two nonconsecutive terms. Seven Republicans were reelected (Lincoln, Grant, McKinley, Eisenhower, Nixon, Reagan, and Bush 43). Of those reelected, Lincoln, McKinley, FDR, and Nixon did not complete their terms (in FDR's case, his fourth). As shown in table 3.3, two Democratic presidents were defeated for reelection

Table 3.3 Winning the Presidency, 1856–2004 (38 elections and reelections)

Feature	Democrats	Republicans
Elected and reelected*	15 (39%)	23 (61%)
Number of persons*	9 (36%)	16 (64%)
Reelected	3 (FDR 3 times)	7
Elected twice non-sequentially	1 (Cleveland)	0
Defeated for reelection	2 (Cleveland, Carter)	4 (B. Harrison, Taft, Hoover, Bush 41)
VPs Succeeding	2 (Truman, L. Johnson)	5 (A. Johnson, Arthur, T. Roosevelt, Coolidge, Ford)
Successors elected to full terms	2 (Truman, L. Johnson)	2 (T. Roosevelt, Coolidge)
Successor defeated for full term	0	1 (Ford)

Source: Compiled by the author from data in Michael Nelson, ed., *Guide to the Presidency*, 2nd ed. (Washington, DC: Congressional Quarterly Press, 1996), 1667–69.

*Does not include A. Johnson, Arthur, or Ford, who were never elected president.

(one, Cleveland, was subsequently elected to a second term) as were four Republicans.

How one is elected may differ significantly, and that variation can have a profound effect on a president's political influence in Washington. The nature and effect of split-party government has been discussed earlier (see table 3.2). Table 3.4 lists those elections since 1856 in which the winner lacked a decisive victory in the popular or electoral vote or both. Several points are notable:

— Over half of the elections (twenty-one of thirty-eight) were close.

— The number of close elections is equally divided between the parties: ten Democrats, eleven Republicans.

— Two-thirds of the presidents in close elections (fourteen of the twenty-one) *did not receive a majority of the popular vote,* including three who lost it (Hayes, Harrison, and Bush 43). These fourteen represent 37 percent of all elections, 1856–2004.

— In one-third of the elections noted in table 3.4 (seven of twenty-one) the winners had slim approval in both the popular and electoral counts. Two presidents lost the popular vote and had bare majorities in the Electoral College (Hayes in 1876 and Bush 43 in 2000). One other, Benjamin Harrison in 1888, also lost the popular vote but won 58 percent of the electoral vote.

— Finally, over two-thirds of these twenty-one presidencies with close elections also faced opposition party control of one or both houses of Congress at some point in their terms (see table 3.2). Additionally, seven of the presidencies with comfortable wins also faced opposition party control on Capitol Hill (Eisenhower twice, Nixon in his second term, Bush 41, Grant, Hoover, and Reagan in his second term).

These numbers are profoundly important for understanding the political status and policy challenges of a presidency in the

Table 3.4 Close Presidential Elections, 1856–2004

Results	Democrats (year)	Republicans (year)
Popular Vote		
Won by plurality (12)	9: Buchanan (1856), Cleveland (1884, 1892), Wilson (1912, 1916), Truman (1948), Kennedy (1960), Clinton (1992, 1996)	3: Lincoln (1860), Garfield (1880); Nixon (1968)
Won by 50 ± 52% (6)	1: Carter (1976)	5: McKinley (1896, 1900), Taft (1908), Reagan (1980), Bush (2004)
Lost (3)	0	3: Hayes (1876), B. Harrison (1888), Bush (2000)
Electoral Vote		
Won by 50 ± 55%* (7)	3: Cleveland (1884), Wilson (1916), Carter (1976)	4: Hayes (1876), McKinley (1900), Bush (2000, 2004)

*These seven elections are the closest during the period, representing those with limited popular and electoral vote support. In two cases, Hayes and Bush 43, the president lost the popular vote.

Source: Compiled from data in Harold W. Stanley and Richard G. Niemi, *Vital Statistics on American Politics*, 3rd ed. (Washington, DC: Congressional Quarterly Press, 1992), 113–15, and Internet sources for recent elections.

separated system. Presidents enter and reenter the White House with variable public endorsements as measured by the special combination of popular and electoral vote, supplemented by the independent results of congressional elections. As shown, more presidents win in close elections and/or are accompanied at some point by an opposition party Congress. Victory for many presidents authorizes a location for exercising power—the White House—but little else by way of political capital at the start. Legitimate occupancy of the office is, unquestionably, an affirmation of position and institutional status. But it is notable that more than half of the presidents, from 1856 to 2004, have had to strengthen their standing virtually from their inauguration forward. Their motivation for doing so is clear enough given that they are held accountable for governing whether or not they have the political resources to rule. The bottom line goes something like this: Being elected president is but the first step in the exercise of power.

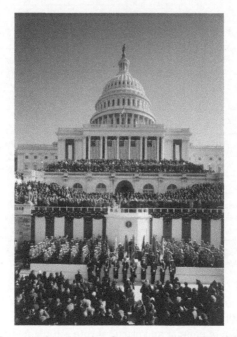

Fig. 3.2. Inauguration: A national ceremony and public celebration for the new or reelected president; in this case President Clinton on January 20, 1993. (Architect of the Capitol, AOC no. 73564)

Becoming President by Other Means

As shown in table 3.3, seven vice presidents have succeeded the president with whom they served. Death was the reason in six cases, resignation in one (Nixon). This total represents 16 percent of all presidents. Five of the seven sought election to a full term, four winning (Truman and Lyndon Johnson among Democrats, Theodore Roosevelt and Coolidge among Republicans) and one losing narrowly (Ford). Succeeding vice presidents have served just over thirty-five years (16 percent of the time, 1789–2005), twenty-eight of those years coming since 1901 (27 percent of the time).

It is true that vice presidents are elected along with presidents, but their selection is typically more akin to an appointment. Presidential nominees choose their running mates, most often based on their assessment of how the selection will aid their election and contribute to their presidency if they win. Vice presidents cannot ordinarily predict whether or when they will move into the Oval Office. Therefore they cannot plan to do so in any serious way. They profit from proximity and from performing whatever tasks presidents assign to them. Recent presidents, at least from Carter to Bush 43, have given the vice presidents serious responsibilities. During this time (1977–2005), three ran for president—Mondale in 1984, Bush 41 in 1988, and Gore in 2000. Only Bush 41 was elected.

Proximity and weighty assignments familiarize vice presidents with the issues and processes of presidential leadership. When the unpredicted happens and vice presidents take the oath of office, they assume leadership of a presidency created and shaped for someone else. Typically it is not possible in the short run to reconstitute the office, cabinet, and other major posts to suit the style and goals of the new president. It is not workable to have wholesale turnover. Why? Because the successor needs staff and agency heads to help with the transition, talented and experienced staff are not immediately available as replacements, and precipitate change will likely be interpreted as a rejection of the departed president. These issues were not as important in earlier times when staffs were small and appointments few. But they are vital in contemporary times. Consequently successors may have to wait until they win a full term before reshaping their predecessor's presidency to suit their style of serving. Four twentieth-century successors have had that opportunity—Theodore Roosevelt, Coolidge, Truman, and Lyndon Johnson.

Conclusion

The Founders designed a unique election system, one so special that it was uncertain exactly how it would work. Presidents were to be elected for four-year terms by electors, not directly by the people. Representatives were to be elected for two-year terms by the people and senators for six-year terms by state legislatures (much later changed to popular election in the Seventeenth Amendment). This modified democratic arrangement has shaped much of national politics, specifying as it does the opportunities and constraints that define presidential power. As described, history abounds with efforts to further democratize how presidents and members of Congress are nominated and elected, with some of these changes incorporated into constitutional amendments (though just one, the Twelfth, changing the Electoral College).

It is evident that the separation of elections and partitioning of terms sustain the separation of powers. Political parties function first and foremost to organize elections, with their committees and leaders operating interdependently throughout the federal system. Just as there is no single, determinative election, so there is no overarching party component. The nature of the system is such that the strength of political parties is measured by their capacity to adapt to differences among regions, state regulations, elected positions, term lengths, and the policy preferences of voters. It is a mark of the maturity of the American system that the same two major parties have existed for 150 years.

Presidents enter the White House under dramatically different political conditions. Some serve with their party having majority status in Congress; many others face opposition party congresses. Slightly more win in close elections, several win by a plurality of the popular vote, and a few have lost the popular vote. The way we elect the national government permits both parties to win, thus forcing presidents to work across the aisle in support of their programs.

Presidential performance is rated more and more frequently by more and more polling outlets. As a consequence, campaigning has become a permanent feature of life in the White House. At one time, the quadrennial election was the principal occasion for a public judgment of presidential performance. Now ratings are rendered many times each month (check realclearpolitics.com for how many). Presidents respond by taking their messages directly to the people.

One-fourth of the twentieth-century presidents first entered without being elected as such. Vice presidents taking over face the special challenge initially of governing within a presidency created to serve someone else. Given that elections are by the calendar, not issue emergence, seeking electoral legitimacy as a replacement president awaits the election year—in the case of Truman nearly four years. This arrangement is yet another variation to account for in analyzing the American presidency and its place in government.

Notes

1. Rhodes Cook, *The Presidential Nominating Process: A Place for Us?* (Lanham, MD: Roman and Littlefield Publishers, 2004), 37.
2. See Charles O. Jones, *The Presidency in a Separated System,* (Washington, DC: Brookings Institution Press, 2005), 136.

3. Samuel Kernell, *Going Public: New Strategies of Presidential Leadership,* 3rd ed. (Washington, DC: Congressional Quarterly Press, 1997).

References

Ceaser, James W. *Presidential Selection: Theory and Development.* Princeton, NJ: Princeton University Press, 1979.

Cook, Rhodes. *The Presidential Nominating Process: A Place for Us?* Lanham, MD: Roman and Littlefield, 2004.

David, Paul T., Ralph M. Goldman, and Richard C. Bain. *The Politics of National Party Conventions.* Washington, DC: Brookings Institution, 1960.

DeGregorio, William A. *The Complete Book of U.S. Presidents.* New York: Gramercy Books, 2005.

Nelson, Michael, ed., *Guide to the Presidency.* 2nd ed. Washington, DC: Congressional Quarterly, 1996.

Stanley, Harold W. and Robert G. Niemi. *Vital Statistics on American Politics.* 3rd ed. Washington, DC: Congressional Quarterly, 1992.

Chapter 4
Making and Remaking
a Presidency

Presidents enter a government already hard at work. A separated powers system is bound to feature differing tenures and work habits among its institutional components. Elected officials come and go, typically in different time frames. Bureaucrats keep on "bureaucrating," judges keep on judging, and lobbyists and journalists are forever.

A change at the top is unquestionably important, but programs and people already in place explain most of what happens in Washington. And the workload grows, as measured by programs administered and dollars spent. It was not until 1962 that national government outlays reached $100 billion. Twenty years later, outlays exceeded $700 billion, and twenty years after that, in 2002, outlays eclipsed the $2 trillion mark. Nine presidents served in these forty years, each inheriting responsibility for the growth experienced by their predecessors.

A huge bureaucracy is required to administer programs costing billions and trillions of dollars. Much of the work is done in the cabinet departments. There were ten of these at the end of World War II in 1945, two of which (War and Navy) were soon folded into a Department of Defense. Five were added in the next sixty years, each one representing new or substantially enhanced federal agendas (for example, health, education, energy, and domestic security). Outlays for the Department of Health and Human Services during the Bush 43 presidency exceeded those for the whole federal government during the Carter presidency, with the Department of Defense not far behind.

Incoming presidents are expected to take charge of this leviathan. They will be held accountable for what takes place in an ever-changing labyrinth of federal units, programs, rules and procedures, and ties to other domestic and foreign governments. As newly elected presidents ponder the tasks of moving in to take charge, they observe others moving out—those with experience in assuming responsibility for the permanent, stay-in-Washington, government employees. Since new presidents and their aides are mostly of a different party than those leaving, little is said in passing. The new team has to learn on the job. And that job is to make a presidency effective enough to accept responsibility for what happens in government. What follows is some of what must be done.

Removing the Caps

Picture several triangles bounded within one large triangle. Now imagine that the caps are removed, thus forming trapezoids. Those geometric images convey what happens with a change at the top. The White House empties out, as do the offices of departmental and agency leaders. The president has a constitutional responsibility to fill many of these positions "by and with the Advice and Consent of the Senate" (Art. II, Sec. 2). During much of the nineteenth century patronage, the appointment of partisans, extended well down into the departments and agencies. A professional civil service was created with the passage of the Pendleton Act (1883), thereafter limiting appointments to the top leadership positions.

The president has several bundles of appointments. Among the most important are the White House staff, cabinet and subcabinet positions, agency heads and other top-level positions, regulatory commissioners, board memberships, and ambassadors and consuls. Federal judicial appointments are also vested in the president but await vacancies. There is no wholesale exit of federal judges with the election of a new president. Presidents also "have the Power to fill up all Vacancies that may happen during the Recess of the Senate" (Art. II, Sec. 2), a provision that permits the president temporarily to appoint officials whose nominations are held up in the Senate.

As noted, patronage was widespread during the first one hundred years, and it is still dominant with major policy positions as well as with a president's personal staff. Thus it is expected that presidents will appoint those who have demonstrated support for the party and its leader. In recent decades, however, there are calls for presidents to appoint at least one member of the other party to the cabinet. Most post–World War II presidents have tried to do so. Thus, for example, Senator William Cohen (R-Maine) served as secretary of defense in the Clinton presidency, and former Representative Norman Mineta (D-California) was appointed secretary of transportation by President George W. Bush (Mineta was secretary of commerce for President Clinton).

Gender, racial, and ethnic diversity has only recently been a standard for evaluating a cabinet. From 1945 to 1977 (Truman through Nixon-Ford), 97 percent of the cabinet secretaries were Caucasian men. Eisenhower appointed one woman, Johnson an African American man, and Ford a woman and African American man. Each of these appointments was a replacement or to lead a newly created department. The original cabinets of all four presidents in this period were white males.

Cabinets during 1977–89 had somewhat more diversity. Carter appointed three women, including one African American. Two of the three were in the original cabinet. Reagan appointed two women and one each African American and Hispanic American males. The African American was in the original cabinet.

Since 1989, diversity in cabinet appointments is a standard by which future presidential appointments will be evaluated. Seventy-six percent of diversity appointments, 1945–2005, were made in this third period: Bush 41 making six such appointments, Clinton sixteen, and Bush 43 thirteen. Caucasian males dominated the first and second periods (97 and 87 percent respectively). They represented just 57 percent of the third.

The number of appointments to the original cabinet also increased substantially: Bush 41 appointing three in his original cabinet, Clinton eight, and Bush 43 seven. In Clinton's case white males were in the minority. They were half of the Bush 43 cabinet. There is no reason to expect a reversal of this trend, given that it represents greater political participation by women and minorities.

Fig. 4.1. President Reagan meets with his cabinet in the Cabinet Room of the White House. (National Archives and Records Administration [ARC 198576])

In another important development, diversity appointments began to be made for top-tier cabinet posts in the Clinton and Bush 43 presidencies. Clinton appointed the first woman as attorney general (Janet Reno) and secretary of state (Madeleine Albright). Bush 43 appointed the first African American male and female as secretaries of state (Colin Powell and Condoleezza Rice) and the first Hispanic American as attorney general (Alberto Gonzalez).

From Campaigning to Governing

Campaigning differs from governing. Here is how a Reagan aide compared the two activities: "[Campaigning] is us versus them. It's Republicans versus Democrats. That's not the same as governing. . . . There aren't many Hail Mary passes in governing. It's chewing up five or ten yards at a time and making people play on your side of the turf." Another presidential aide explained campaigning as a "one-ring circus," focused as it is on the candidate and a day certain when a winner is declared. Government, by contrast, is a "thousand-ring circus."[1]

That the two activities are different does not mean that they are unrelated. A presidential campaign determines which team will govern, and influences how they will do so. Campaigns typically offer competing policy priorities or policy proposals where candidates agree on priorities. Candidates and their staffs create and manage a national organization and often intersect congressional and gubernatorial campaigns. Thus candidates have an opportunity to learn about policy themes, preferences of others, capabilities of staff, and organizational effectiveness. It is in these senses that campaigning has the potential of preparing the winner to govern.

It is also the case that governing influences the campaign. Candidates conduct issue searches in the course of their travels. Most issues emerge from what government is presently doing. For example, the 2004 presidential campaign focused on the war on terrorism and in Iraq, home security, energy resources, Social Security, deficits, and taxes. Accordingly, governing during Bush 43's first term set the campaign agenda, and the two candidates tested public reactions to these issues. The winner (Bush 43 by a narrow margin) then applied the lessons learned to governing in his second term.

Meanwhile, members of Congress conducted mostly separate campaigns, with issues customized to their state and local constituencies. The effect of presidents and congresses applying the lessons of campaigns to governing sets a new agenda for the next election. These two functions—governing and campaigning—are truly and continually interrelated, just as one might expect in a representative democracy.

At one time presidents were reluctant to travel extensively to build support for their programs. There were examples, notably the national tour of Woodrow Wilson in favor of the League of Nations. More common were fund-raising trips and radio or television addresses. President Johnson observed: "Sometimes . . . the only way to reach the papers and the people was to pick a fight with the Congress, to say mean words and show my temper." Mostly he believed he should "work from within" because going outside might alienate members of Congress.[2]

But in 1965 Johnson had the advantages of a landslide win and huge Democratic majorities in Congress. No president since has had such a favorable political position. As a result, and with developments in communication, presidents have increasingly reached out to the public in building support. To aid in this task, presidents bring campaign consultants into office with them. The most recent example is Karl Rove for Bush 43, serving as deputy chief of staff and advising the president in regard to both policy and electoral campaigns. Not surprisingly, Rove has been the target of vigorous criticism, as will future political consultants taking jobs in the White House. Why? They represent a fusion of campaigning and governing that many critics believe should be separate.

Getting Started: The Transition

Presidents-elect have approximately ten weeks to form and prepare their presidencies. In that time they set policy priorities; make critical appointments; establish connections with Congress, the bureaucracy, the press, and other governments; and prepare to move into empty offices in the White House and other government buildings. It is an enormously complex undertaking, one commonly involving a switch of parties when a new president is elected (seven party switches of eight transitions in the post–World War II period). Setting priorities normally follows from what was proposed during the campaign. After all, campaigns are about agendas. They form the basis of the overall debate. It is true, however, that elections by the calendar rather than issue emergence can result in substantial variation in the sequence of priorities. No one doubted that ending the war in Vietnam was a priority for Nixon in 1968, or that energy and government ethics took precedence for Carter in 1976. The economy was paramount for Reagan in 1980 and again for Clinton in 1992 ("The economy, stupid"). Much less clear were the priorities for Bush 41 in 1988 when the campaign was criticized for lacking issues or for Bush 43 in 2000 when several issues were debated but no one issue stood out with the public as a priority. Bush himself designated tax cuts as paramount. Having a clear theme is a distinct advantage in transitioning into the government because it sets the purpose and direction of a presidency, as well as aiding in deciding whom to appoint.

Media attention during the transition understandably focuses on critical appointments. There is strong interest in filling in the boxes, those key cabinet posts and the principal staff aides to the president. The transition is an anxious time for many campaign aides who anticipate appointments. And interest runs high among groups that do business with the government, as well as congressional committees and their staffs who will be working with the White House and cabinet departments. Table 4.1 shows the present-day cabinet departments and the secretaries, plus the attorney general, in the fall, 2006.

Certain practices and sequences have developed for making appointments, most of which are effectively implemented if there has been transition planning prior to the election itself. Among these rules are the following: select an appointments chief with federal government experience, act fast, appoint White House staff and major cabinet posts (State, Treasury, Defense, Justice) as early as feasible, quickly settle the futures of close advisers, let appointments speak for policy, and separate the functions of dismantling the campaign from those of managing appointments. Taken together these practices amount to clear-headed and logical planning for a takeover, one in which program and personnel are sufficiently coordinated as to convey a well-defined sense of mission. Measured by these standards, the Kennedy (1960), Reagan (1980), and Bush 43 (2000) transitions received high marks, the Carter (1976), Bush 41 (1988), and especially Clinton (1992) transitions low marks. A smooth transition does not guarantee an effective presidency, but it does make more likely an effective beginning.

"Innocent until nominated," is how C. Boyden Gray, counsel to Bush 41, described the appointment process. Paul C. Light, an expert on presidential appointments, has stated that "the appointment process itself has been the most significant barrier" to convincing quality executives to enter government.[3] Nominees are subject to background checks by the Federal Bureau of Investigation, elaborate financial disclosure forms, reviews by Senate committee staff, questioning in confirmation hearings, and scrutiny by the media and interest groups. All of this examination takes time. Delay in filling critical posts, especially at the

Table 4.1 Cabinet Departments and Those Serving in 2006 Cabinet

Department	Created	Serving in 2006 (No.)*
State	1789	Condoleezza Rice (64th)
Treasury	1789	Henry Paulson (74th)
Defense	1789 as War; 1798 as Navy; 1947 as Defense	Donald Rumsfeld (21st as Defense)
Justice	1792 as Attorney General; 1870 as Justice	Alberto Gonzalez (79th as Attorney General)
Interior	1849	Dirk Kempthorne (49th)
Agriculture	1889 as cabinet level	Michael Johanns (29th)
Labor	1913 (originally Commerce and Labor, 1903)	Elaine Lan Chao (24th)
Commerce	1913 (originally Commerce and Labor, 1903)	Carlos Guticrrcz (36th)
Health and Human Services	1953 as Health, Education, and Welfare; 1979 as HHS	Michael Leavitt (20th as HEW; 8th as HHS)
Housing and Urban Development	1965	Alphonso Jackson (13th)
Transportation	1966	Mary E. Peters (15th)
Energy	1977	Samuel Bodman (11th)
Education	1979	Margaret Spellings (8th)

(*continued*)

Table 4.1 (*continued*)

Department	Created	Serving in 2006 (No.)*
Veterans Affairs	1988	Jim Nicholson (6th)
Homeland Security	2002	Michael Chertoff (2nd)

*Does not count individuals twice if they served more than one president in the position.

Source: Compiled by the author from information in *The United States Government Manual, 2005–2006* (Washington, DC: Government Printing Office, 2005).

Fig. 4.2. Transition from one generation to the next—Eisenhower to Kennedy. (**Dwight D. Eisenhower Library**)

subcabinet level, complicates an already challenging task for a new president in assuming responsibility for governing.

Partisanship too can add to the trials of a new administration. It is generally conceded that presidents should be able to appoint the people they want. Therefore the Senate consents to most appointments. More often than not in recent decades, however, the president has had to get consent from a Senate controlled by the other party (the case at different times for Nixon, Ford, Reagan, Bush 41, Clinton, and Bush 43). Accordingly, presidents have had to consider the possibility that a nominee will be rejected, as, for example, was the high profile nomination of former Senator John Tower (R-Texas) to be secretary of defense in the Bush 41 cabinet. Remarkably, many of his former colleagues in the Senate voted against Tower. Interestingly, next in line for Bush 41 was Richard Cheney, who later served with Bush's son as vice president.

Although of a different order, judicial appointments, too, have come to be very contentious. These appointments are not a part of building a presidency. Rather they represent an exercise of the president's constitutional authority in the case of "Judges of the supreme Court" (Art. II, Sec. 1) and as designated by law in the cases of judges for "inferior Courts" (Art. III, Sec. 1). These appointments are to fill vacancies in the third branch and are essentially life terms, not coincident with a president's time in office.

As with executive appointments, most of the president's judicial choices are approved. But split-party control between the president and the Senate has made the process of "advice and consent" increasingly stressful, particularly for the courts of appeals and the Supreme Court. Appointments may be held up in the Committee on the Judiciary or, rarely, defeated on the Senate floor. In the 108th Congress (2003–05), the minority-party Democrats employed the filibuster to thwart several Bush 43 appointments to the courts of appeals, a practice halted at least temporarily by a bipartisan agreement in the 109th Congress (2005–07).

Turnover: Remaking a Presidency

Having formed a presidency, achieved the consent of the Senate for the cabinet, and fitted the new team into the permanent government of long-serving bureaucrats, a high incumbent-return Congress, and life-term judges, presidents can only hope that their presidencies will cohere effectively. There are no guarantees. Those appointed typically come from very different backgrounds. In parliamentary systems the cabinet is typically made up of ministers with similar political experiences—mostly as members of parliament. Not so in the separated system of the United States. Cabinet secretaries have varied backgrounds in the public and private spheres. For example, the first cabinets of Clinton and Bush 43 were drawn from business and banking, law, Congress, education, state and local governments, and the military. Most will not have worked together in the past; a few may not even be well acquainted with the president. The challenge is to insure that a disparate set of department heads support the president's programs and know how to put them in place.

The White House staff typically does have a common political experience. Most will have been active in the campaign just ended. It is rare for these campaign aides to be appointed to the first cabinet. They are, however, intimately familiar with the president's programs and how they were developed during the campaign. They are, therefore, well qualified to monitor how and whether proposals are being processed and promoted within the departments and agencies, at least those with experience enough to know their way around Washington.

It is not uncommon for conflicts to develop between these staff persons and department and agency heads, or for both sets to be at odds with senior bureaucrats. Reference is sometimes made to presidential appointees "going native" as they settle into their positions in the departments and agencies. The concern is that they will express more allegiance to existing programs than to the president's agenda for change.

Serving a president is a temporary job. After all, the Twenty-second Amendment sets a two-term limitation on presidential service.

Few cabinet secretaries serve two full terms, just ten since the ratification of the term-limitation amendment in 1951: Eisenhower, two; Kennedy-Johnson, three; Reagan, one; and Clinton, four. Turnover is high, though variable, among presidents. The median number of months served by cabinet secretaries for two-term administrations (including those where a vice president took over, such as Kennedy-Johnson and Nixon-Ford) varies from forty-eight months for Clinton's eight years to twenty-four months for the Nixon-Ford eight years. The Nixon and Ford presidencies had a total of forty-three cabinet secretarial appointments; Eisenhower had just twenty. Remarkably there were five attorneys general and five secretaries of labor serving Nixon and Ford, an average of just over nineteen months for these two sets.

What explains these significant differences in turnover? Certainly a shift in presidents (as with Kennedy's death and Nixon's resignation) can be expected to produce turnover as the takeover presidents eventually bring in their own teams. In Nixon's case, however, there was a pattern of high turnover even before he resigned. Appointing people to the right job at the start appears to be important in their retention. Related is a good working relationship with the president and the White House staff. Even where these conditions are met, however, turnover is relatively high. The jobs are demanding, criticism is inevitable, and the pay is relatively low. Thus it is that high-profile persons often prefer to return to more rewarding positions in the private sphere.

The Clinton and Bush 43 presidencies suggest that change may be under way. The Clinton cabinet had among the lowest turnover of any eight-year presidency in the twentieth century and the highest number serving the full eight years. The Bush 43 cabinet set a modern record for the fewest resignations in a first term, a turnover of just two cabinet secretaries—one voluntarily, one involuntarily. That record was then followed by another—the highest number of changes in the cabinet between the first and second terms. Perhaps turnover in the future will be lessened with greater stability a result. That outcome is surely to be welcomed because frequent changes at the top result in having to reestablish connections between the bureaucracy and the White House, Congress, the states, and other governments.

First and Second Terms

First and second terms are very different. The pressures are intense in the first term to make appointments that will meet the expectations of campaign workers and contributors, members of Congress, interest groups, party organizations, and the media. Each appointment is evaluated for what it reveals about the emerging presidency in policy and political terms.

Second term appointments also receive attention, but the situation is markedly different. Certain key personnel may decide to continue, the president has somewhat greater flexibility in filling vacancies, and the pool of potential nominees will include several who either have experience in the department or agency or have earned the president's confidence in performing other related jobs.

Eight presidents were reelected (1896–2004): McKinley, Wilson, Franklin Roosevelt three times, Eisenhower, Nixon, Reagan, Clinton, and Bush 43. Their records show that renewal of the cabinet at the point of reelection is a modern phenomenon. The first set of four—McKinley, Wilson, Roosevelt in his second term, and Eisenhower—made no changes at the point of their reelections. Roosevelt did have a single change in each of his second and third reelections (1940 and 1944).

The second set of four—Nixon, Reagan, Clinton, and Bush 43—made major changes at the point of reelection. In 1972 Nixon asked for the resignations of the White House staff and the cabinet. "There are no sacred cows. . . . We will tear up the pea patch," Nixon reportedly said to his staff.[4] Six changes were made in the cabinet (50 percent turnover), and the staff was reorganized. Reagan matched Nixon in making six changes; Clinton appointed five new cabinet secretaries, and Bush 43 set an all-time record with eight changes. In the latter three instances, the shifts were explained more by preferences of the cabinet secretaries than by a Nixon-style house cleaning. Still the effect was a renewal of each of the three presidencies, with an average turnover of 45 percent.

It is frequently stated that there is a second-term curse, suggesting that reelected presidents are bound to fail. The rationale for this observation is that much of a president's program is enacted in the first term, that Washington insiders consider a second-term president a "lame duck," and a laxness develops that encourages scandal. A brief review of the historical record suggests that what happens in the second term is more circumstantially than historically determined. The number of reelected presidents in the modern era is small. It becomes smaller as one reviews each case.

McKinley was assassinated, and Wilson had a severe stroke within a year of their reelections. Roosevelt was reelected three times, thus making it difficult to argue he was cursed. Nixon resigned in the second year of his second term as a consequence of the Watergate investigation. Bush 43 had not completed his second term at this writing. That leaves three pure cases: Eisenhower, Reagan, and Clinton.

Each of the three did have scandals but of very different sorts. Eisenhower's chief of staff, Sherman Adams, had sought to influence federal agencies on behalf of a businessman, Bernard Goldfine, from whom Adams had accepted gifts. Adams resigned his post. The principal Reagan scandal involved a complicated scheme by which the profits from covert sales of arms to Iran were diverted to the contras seeking to overthrow the leftist government in Nicaragua. The president accepted responsibility, Chief of Staff Donald Regan was replaced, and a shakeup of the national security staff followed.

The Clinton scandal in the second term involved personal behavior on the part of the president. He was already the subject of an investigation by an independent counsel, Kenneth Starr, in regard to a land deal in Arkansas and accusations regarding sexual advances to one Paula Jones. The new scandal in 1998 involved revelations regarding a relationship with a White House intern, Monica Lewinsky. Starr's report to the House of Representatives resulted in the president's impeachment by a largely partisan vote in the House of Representatives. However, his trial in the Senate did not result in his removal.

Did these second-term scandals wreck the presidencies in each case? The evidence is not conclusive enough to generalize about a "curse." Four factors are relevant: the timing of the scandal, the job approval rankings of the president, mid-term election results, and production of major legislation. Here are the facts:

— Eisenhower: The scandal was revealed in 1958 (Adams resigned just prior to the mid-term election) the president's job-approval ratings had been declining prior to the scandal and increased after, Democrats had huge gains in both the House and Senate in 1958, and there were slightly more major pieces of legislation passed in the second term over the first term.

— Reagan: The scandal was revealed in 1987, carrying over to 1988; the president's job-approval ratings declined prior to the scandal, then increased to the end of his term; Democrats recaptured control of the Senate and had slight net increases in the House *prior to* the scandal; and second-term production of major legislation was substantially greater than in the first term (with the highest two-year output in 1987–88).

— Clinton: The Lewinsky scandal was revealed early in 1998, carrying over to the Senate trial in 1999; the president's job-approval ratings increased after inauguration in 1997, declined moderately in 1998, then increased toward the end of his second term; defying the so-called "sixth-year itch," Democrats actually had a slight net gain of House seats in 1998 and no net loss in the Senate; and substantially less major legislation was enacted in the second over the first term.

In summary, these mixed results make it difficult to take a broad view of second terms. Scandals are not that closely associated either with job-approval ratings or election outcomes. Major legislation can be and is enacted during second terms, sometimes in greater numbers than in first terms. A more supportable conclusion than that implied by a second-term curse is that a host of variables combine to influence the workings and production of a separated powers system, much as one would expect from the way the Founders designed the government. It is useful to be reminded that the original design had no term limit and therefore no structural basis for a "lame-duck" president.

Conclusion

The presidency is a dynamic institution, one constantly being shaped and reshaped. Two major factors aid in understanding this vitality, both associated with its democratic base. First, presidents enter and leave, actually rather frequently as it happens. They are given latitude in forming their presidencies within certain bounds. If reelected they have the option of reshaping, perhaps revitalizing, their organization and programs. Second, the presidency is purposely and historically representative. Accordingly, one may expect responsiveness to events in the form of organizational and programmatic adjustments.

Institutional dynamism does not imply instability or radical change. Indeed, the separation of powers is designed to thwart dramatic reshaping of the structure and organization of the executive branch. Presidents do make adjustments that may then be incorporated into future White House operations. The presidency has undergone evolutionary change in the last half century, as will be shown in chapters 6 and 7. Typically, however, the shifts reflect social, economic, and technological changes, much as one would expect in a representative democracy.

Notes

1. Quoted in Charles O. Jones, *Passages to the Presidency: From Campaigning to Governing* (Washington, DC: Brookings Institution Press, 1998), 52.
2. Lyndon B. Johnson, *Vantage Point: Perspectives on the Presidency, 1963–1969* (New York: Holt, Rinehart and Winston, 1971), 450.
3. Light quoted in Charles Babington, "Presidential Appointment Process Questioned," *Washington Post*, January 10, 2001.
4. As reported in Stephen E. Ambrose, *Nixon: Ruin and Recover, 1973–1990* (New York: Simon and Schuster, 1991), 14.

References

Burke, John P. *The Institutional Presidency*. Baltimore, MD: Johns Hopkins University Press, 1992.

Cohen, Jeffrey E. *The Politics of the U.S. Cabinet*. Pittsburgh: University of Pittsburgh Press, 1988.

Jones, Charles O. *Passages to the Presidency: From Campaigning to Governing*. Washington, DC: Brookings Institution Press, 1998.

Kumar, Martha Joynt, and Terry Sullivan, eds. *The White House World: Transition, Organization, and Office Operations*. College Station: Texas A&M University Press, 2003.

Pfiffner, James P. *The Strategic Presidency: Hitting the Ground Running*. 2nd ed. Lawrence: University Press of Kansas, 1996.

Chapter 5
Connecting to and Leading the Government

Fair warning: some matters are too important to be interesting. Chapters 5 and 6 are chockful of such topics—organization, management, liaison, policy development, lawmaking, and budgeting. Please persevere. I have sought to make the treatment readable. There is nothing I can do about the importance of such subjects given the Founders' design of a separated system. They were aware of the need for leadership but wary of the ease of control. Therefore what follows in these next two chapters is a recounting of the challenges facing presidents as they endeavor to meet expectations of leadership beyond given powers. Come to think of it, that sounds interesting as well as important.

The opening sentence of Article II, "The executive Power shall be vested in a President of the United States of America," might well have included the following phrase: "who will be responsible for connecting to the rest of the government." The Founders created a government of parts. As the only nationally elected leader and chief of the bureaucratic branch, it was inevitable that the president would be held accountable for all parts. That fact alone is a stimulus for presidential attentiveness to what happens throughout government.

And what a government it has become. *The United States Government Manual, 2005-2006* lists the following units for the executive branch (apart from the Executive Office of the President [EOP] to be discussed subsequently): fifteen cabinet departments; fifty-nine independent establishments and government corporations, fifty-one boards, commissions, and committees; four quasi-official agencies, and numerous multi- and bilateral organizations. And these agencies are but the tips of many icebergs. For example, the Department of Defense has three departments, one for each of the services, sixteen agencies, and numerous commands and field activities. The recently created Department of Homeland Security has two assistant secretaries, seven directors, one deputy secretary, five undersecretaries, and a commandant of the Coast Guard. There are independent organizational units in the executive branch on futures trading, product safety, arts and humanities, postal rates, transportation safety, to name but a few.

Organizations manage people, millions of people in the case of the national government. Table 5.1 shows how many. The total federal employment, civilian and military, approaches 4 million— approximately the size of the city of Los Angeles. Table 5.1 also shows the number of elected officials in Washington. Note that the number of legislators increased as reflecting the addition of states for the Senate and the increase in population for the House of Representatives until it was capped at 435 in 1911. The number on the executive side stayed at one president and one vice president. Now look at the number of employees: millions to be managed by the two elected executives; more than thirty thousand for legislators.

But guess what? The number of federal employees has actually decreased in recent years for several reasons. More of the work of the federal government is now done at the state and local levels, where the number of employees has increased by 40 percent in the last twenty years (now approaching 20 million). It is also the case that work formerly done by government employees is now often contracted out to private firms. And military service is now

Table 5.1 Federal Employment, 2003

Branch	Employees, 2003	
Executive: Civilian	2,677,294	
Executive: Military	1,045,067*	
Legislative	31,297	
Judicial	34,472	
Total	3,788,130	

Elected Officials	1789	2006
Executive	2	2
Legislative: House	65 (13 states)	435 (50 states)
Legislative: Senate	26 (13 states)	100 (50 states)
Judicial	0	0

Source: *Statistical Abstract of the United States: 2004–2005* (Washington, DC: Government Printing Office, 2005), 322, 331

*For 2002.

voluntary (not conscripted) and "high tech." These developments reduce the number of employees but increase the management and accountability issues. Federal programs like Medicaid or crime control may be directed at lower levels of government, but the president will still be held responsible for results.

Cost too justifies attention by presidents to making connections. The numbers are staggering and appear to escalate in spite of efforts to control expenditures. Table 5.2 provides statistics for recent decades. Previously unimagined deficits have contributed to an overall debt of epic proportions. The figures represent billions of dollars, meaning that many entries are in the trillions. Money coming in actually exceeded outlays in 2000, a remarkable achievement representing an economic boom at the end of the

Table 5.2 Expenditures, Deficits, and Debt (in billions of dollars)

Budget Features	Year 1980	1990	2000	2004 (est)
Receipts	517.1	1,032.0	2,025.2	1,798.1
Outlays	590.9	1,253.2	1,788.8	2,313.8
Surplus or deficit	−73.8	−221.2	+236.4	−520.7
Outlays as % of GDP	21.7	21.8	18.4	20.2
Gross federal debt	909.0	3,206.3	5,628.7	7,486.4
Debt as % of GDP	33.4	55.9	58.0	65.3

GDP = Gross Domestic Product

Source: *Statistical Abstract of the United States 2004–2005* (Washington, DC: Government Printing Office, 2005), 308.

century. Even still the gross federal debt continued to rise. Receipts more than tripled from 1980 to 2004, but outlays quadrupled. Yet outlays as a percent of Gross Domestic Product (GDP), a standard measure of the economy, have remained near 20 percent. More troubling is the mounting total debt as it continues to climb into the trillions and has grown from one-third of GDP to two-thirds.

How much is a trillion? It is very hard to illustrate in human terms but someone once calculated the weight in dollar bills of the debt when it was 1.5 trillion as equivalent to fifteen aircraft carriers, twelve destroyers, two battleships, two cruisers, and seventeen smaller ships combined. At this writing, the gross debt is on its way to 8 trillion. You can do the math. Talk about the need for Weight Watchers!

For present purposes, the numbers in Table 5.2 point up the urgency for presidents to reach into the permanent government in their effort to exercise executive power. Existing programs have the force of the organization that administers them and the clienteles they serve. A new president is already behind schedule in managing this behemoth. The outgoing president and staff formed the budget in place and prepared the next fiscal year's spending and taxing plans. Yet the effects of spending and implementing what is on the books soon will be on the new leader's "watch."

Connecting to Whom?

To whom or what must presidents connect? However much they are held responsible for what happens, the fact is that presidential direction and control over other governing parts varies substantially. For some segments presidents hire and fire, reorganize to an extent, and exercise budgetary power. Other segments have varying degrees of independence, ranging from their own sources of legitimacy to the strength of public or clientele support. The categories—from most White House control to least—are these: cabinet departments and other agencies with appointments coterminous with the president's term or at his pleasure, independent agencies with overlapping and lengthy terms, the other branches of the national government, the media, and other governments and international organizations.

Cabinet Departments and Major Agencies

It is generally conceded that presidents have the right to manage the large departments and agencies. After all, presidents have the gold standard of legitimacy in a democracy—their election. Presidents appoint secretaries, administrators, and directors who are then expected to put into effect presidential policy preferences. Centralized budget control and clearance of program initiatives are levers used by presidents to enforce their decisions. Those failing to satisfy the president can be removed. Recent examples: Secretary of Defense Les Aspin was removed by President Clinton early in his presidency, Secretary of the Treasury Paul O'Neill was fired by President George W. Bush.

Independent Commissions

Congress has established several commissions for policy areas judged to be better placed beyond partisan influences. Most deal with economic and regulatory issues: securities exchange, banking, interest rates, trade, shipping, communications, labor relations. Paramount among these is the Federal Reserve System, the "Fed," for the impact of its interest rate decisions on the economy. Presidents make appointments but cannot normally remove commissioners, whose terms overlap so as to provide continuity and usually exceed a president's single term of four years. Bipartisan representation is required on these commissions, with neither party permitted to have an advantage of more than one. Presidents can influence policy through their appointments, but often the greater threats to their independence are the consequences of their favoring the very industries they are charged to regulate.

The Other Branches

Life terms for federal judges are the principal bases for the independence of the judiciary, bolstered by the common belief that elected officials should not influence individual court decisions. Presidents have their chance to affect the direction of courts with their constitutional prerogative of nominating judges, as do senators during the "advice and consent" process in that chamber. Federal court appointments have become increasingly contentious in recent decades with the frequency of split-party government and narrow margins. Since 1968 Republican presidents have had, by far, the most chances to make court appointments, having occupied the White House for twenty-eight of the forty years during that time (1968–2008). There are, however, several cases where judges presumed to be of one philosophical persuasion turned out quite differently (for example, on the Supreme Court, Byron White, a Kennedy appointee, thought to be moderate to liberal yet served as a moderate to conservative justice; John Paul Stevens, a Ford appointee, and David Souter, a Bush 41 appointee, just the opposite).

There is no expectation that presidents will cease influencing Congress. Rather, the challenge is to establish connections with elaborate and differentiated organizations in the House and Senate. The committees and subcommittees in each chamber are an approximate replication of the programmatic structure in the executive (for example, the Department of Defense and the House and Senate Committees on Armed Services). Therefore, connections already exist between the bureaus and their counterpart committees, two of the three legs of what has been termed the "cozy little triangle" (the third leg being the private and clientele interests affected by the issue at hand). Somehow presidents anxious to change policies have to find a way to override these lasting associations by developing close ties of their own with lawmakers (to include committee and subcommittee permanent staff).

Just as important is the need to develop strong relationships with party leaders, including knowledge of what these leaders need by way of White House support for building majorities on legislation. In some instances, the president's party in Congress will have just experienced years of policy strife with an opposition party president. For example, when Kennedy and Clinton were inaugurated, Democrats had been in the majority in the House and Senate for six years during the Eisenhower and Reagan-Bush presidencies. Likewise, Republicans had had House and Senate majorities for six years during the Clinton presidency when Bush 43 entered office. Having honed their skills at opposing the White House, the president's party on Capitol Hill had to become cheerleaders—not always an easy transformation, yet one that may be eased by an adroit presidential staff.

Media

There is a perpetual tension between two vital institutions: the presidency and the press. "Sooner or later, all presidents blame the problems on the media, and they are right. The press and the president are linked in a natural enmity. They need each other and they resent that."[1] The two institutions are naturally competitive, even combative. Presidents are representatives of the people by virtue of their having been elected. Reporters believe that it is their professional, even constitutional, first amendment obligation to inform the people of presidential doings. There are few more sensitive relationships in national politics. The White House press corps is a group of reporters from the print and electronic media who work in the president's house and meet the president's travel schedule. The White House communications operations provide daily briefings and manage alternative outlets for informing the public of national policy decisions. The press secretary comes to be a familiar spokesperson for presidential policy decisions.

Other Governments

The federal government is intricately connected to governance in the fifty states and thousands of localities. According to the 2002 Bureau of the Census count, there were over 87,500 local governmental units (counties, municipalities, townships, and special districts), the overwhelming number receiving and spending federal funds.

In 2003 federal grants-in-aid to state and local governments totaled nearly 400 billion dollars, constituting approximately one-third of all expenditures by those governments. Over 85 percent of this money was for Medicaid, income security, transportation, and education—programs at the core of state and local governance. Spending for some programs is growing at alarming rates: grants for Medicaid from 14 billion in 1980 to 161 billion in 2003; income security from 18 to 86 billion in that same period.

Presidents wishing to reduce or reform these programs have to plan carefully given the investment of the federal government in the social and economic life of states and localities. They need to take advantage of the connections between federal departments and the governments actually administering the programs in preparing proposals for change. They can be guaranteed that members of Congress, all elected from states and congressional districts, will be attentive to the effects of reforms. In fact, it is at this level that government can become very personal for individuals and families, with their responses to changes a predictable result, often as resistance. It is relevant in this regard that presidents who have served as governors, four of the five (1976–2008), are more likely to be sensitive to these needs.

Connecting with foreign governments and international organizations is of a different order. Several cabinet departments (notably Commerce, Defense, Labor, and Treasury) have regular contact with counterparts in other countries, but the Department of State is the primary agency for maintaining relations outside the United States. Presidents appoint ambassadors, who become their personal representatives, but most of those staffing the embassies and other diplomatic missions around the world are Foreign Service personnel, with one at each location designated as Chief of Mission. Likewise, other countries maintain embassies in Washington, DC, essentially their place of contact in the United States.

The Department of State is also the agency responsible for sustaining our relations with international organizations, working through its Bureau of International Organizations. The Permanent Representative to the United Nations is located at the United States Mission in New York and works in conjunction with the Secretary of State.

As is evident, the president's reach into these organizations, branches, and governments is achieved through appointments. But, tension between appointees from the outside and long-serving bureaucrats on the inside is common and understandable. Often the friction is between experts and politicians.

Bureaucrats learn to serve presidents and their associates. The challenge for presidents is to take advantage of bureaucratic experience in formulating and promoting their programs.

Accomplishing this goal can be especially difficult in foreign policy and national security policy. Domestic bureaucracies are located mostly in the United States; foreign and national security policy bureaucracies are located in the United States and throughout the world. Further, differences in attitude and style typically arise between diplomats and the military, thus creating an added form of tension to be managed by presidents.

Can It Be Done?

"The plain fact is that no modern president has fully managed the executive branch. . . . Additionally, presidents fail as managers because they seem to have little appetite for that task, and their interests lie elsewhere."[2] This analysis by a prominent student of public management introduces another element: whether presidents are up to the task of serving effectively as chief executive.

The problem of getting more help for the president was officially recognized in 1937 with a report from a President's Committee on Administrative Management. Its conclusion: "The President needs help."[3] Two years later the Executive Office of the President (EOP) was created. In essence, this action produced an institutional home for units to facilitate information gathering and policy control. Over time the EOP was bound to enlarge its functions and staff, not unlike the bureaucracy it was created to control. What began as a few advisers has grown into many hundreds of staff organized into the major policy areas represented by federal government programs. The present-day EOP is a microcosm of the permanent executive branch.

Table 5.3 shows the EOP organizational units as they existed for the Bush 43 presidency. Note that just two of the units were a part of the EOP in 1939—the White House Office (WHO) and the Office of Management and Budget (OMB) (then as the Bureau of the Budget).[4] Two exceedingly important councils were created in the immediate post–World War II period: the Council of

Table 5.3 Executive Office of the President, 2006

Unit	Created By	Year
White House Office	Executive Order	1939
Office of the Vice President	Constitutional Official	1960s–1970s staff growth
Council of Economic Advisers	Employment Act	1946
Council on Environmental Quality	National Environmental Protection Act	1969
National Security Council	National Security Act	1947
Office of Administration	Executive Order	1977
Office of Management and Budget	Reorganization Plan No. 1 (as the Bureau of the Budget)	1939
Office of National Drug Control Policy	National Narcotics Leadership Act	1988
Office of Policy Development		
—Domestic Policy Council	Executive Order	1993
—National Economic Council	Executive Order	1993
Office of Science and Technology Policy	National Science and Technology Policy Organization and Priorities Act	1971
Office of the U.S. Trade Representative	Executive Order	1963

Source: *The United States Government Manual, 2006-2006* (Government Printing Office, 2005), 85–98.

Economic Advisers (CEA) and the National Security Council (NSC). The remaining six were established from 1963 forward.

The major policy areas are covered by these EOP units: the economy, national security and foreign policy, trade, environmental issues, science and technology, the domestic agenda, and the budget. The units serve several purposes. Some are advisory only (CEA, Council on Environmental Quality, and Office of Science and Technology Policy). Others have responsibilities for coordinating major policy decisions (NSC, the Domestic Policy and National Economic Councils). Two of the units have policymaking functions: the Offices of National Drug Control Policy and the U.S. Trade Representative. The Office of Administration performs primarily housekeeping functions.

That leaves OMB and the WHO, the most important units of all (the Office of the Vice President merits separate treatment below). OMB is a super-coordinating agency. Its list of functions is awesome: prepare and administer the budget, review government effectiveness and recommend organizational changes, clear legislative proposals from departments and agencies, evaluate government performance, and develop regulatory reform proposals.[5] I have advised many students that if they want to have influence in government, get hired by OMB.

Presidents vary in the extent to which they rely on OMB, but none believes that a presidency can work effectively without its experience and expertise. Since 1974, Congress has had a counterpart agency, the Congressional Budget Office, and House and Senate Committees on the Budget. These developments have facilitated connections between the branches on this vital function.

The Inner Circle

The WHO is the inner circle of White House aides, those upon whom the president relies for in-house advice and counsel. These people constitute the "team," those whom the president trusts, often because they have fought the election wars and/or served with the president in prior positions. Many of them will have come to Washington with the president, for example, Georgians who served with Governor Carter, Californians with Reagan, Arkansans with Clinton, and Texans with Bush 43. At best, these aides come to think like the presidents they serve and to understand what is in their president's best interests. At worst, they become arrogant "know it alls" poorly serving the president and the country.

Close identity with the president can protect presidential power by enabling the staff to be sensitive to the future effects of present decisions. Most effective are those aides who warn as well as inform. Position, the status of being president, does not make the holder supreme. Therefore, staff can be enormously helpful by being critical as well as analytical. Least helpful is for staff persons to serve their own egos.

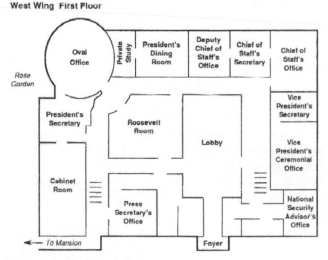

West Wing First Floor

Fig. 5.1 West Wing of the White House, where the president and the inner circle work. (GlobalSecurity.org)

Table 5.4 provides a summary of the contemporary staffing arrangements in the WHO. Presidents have wide discretion in judging how to organize White House operations. Some like Kennedy and Carter preferred open access to the Oval Office, not wishing to have a chief of staff. Others like Eisenhower and Nixon preferred more control through a chief of staff. Reagan worked initially with a "troika," although one of the three, James Baker, was the chief of staff. Clinton, Bush 41, and Bush 43 wanted both: a chief of staff and substantial access for other aides.[6]

The policy issues brought into the White House Office will also vary, depending on the national agenda and the preferences of the president. Notice in the case of Bush 43 (see table 5.4) that homeland security and faith-based and community initiatives merited posts in the WHO. For Clinton, performance review or "reinventing government" was a priority. Lyndon Johnson wanted the poverty program to be located in the White House for the express purpose of highlighting it. Of course, national security is standard for all inner circles.

The management functions are less variable, though they continue to expand. It is the responsibility of many of these aides to establish and maintain the connections that have been the subject of this chapter. Apart from the internal management functions (for example, chief of staff, staff secretary, personnel) most activities involve liaison: legislative, media, cabinet, public, state and local governments. In fact, much of the work of the WHO can be labeled "communications." Presidents work at initiating and maintaining contact and conversations with governmental and public audiences, a task made more complicated by dramatic changes in how information is transmitted and received.

Presidents often have special consultants whose formal position is unlikely to reveal the influence such persons exercise. Typically these confidants' advice is more politically than policy oriented, but it is often difficult to separate the two. Recent advances

Table 5.4 The White House Office Staff Positions, 2006

Title and Area	Number	Responsibilities
Assistant to the president (Management)	9	Chief of staff, deputy chief of staff (2), press secretary, staff secretary, communications, legislative affairs, personnel, speechmaking
Assistant to the president (Special)	1	Chief of staff to the vice president
Assistant to the president (Policy)	5	National Security (2), Faith-Based and Community Initiatives, Homeland Security, Policy and Strategic Planning
Counsel (Law)	1	Legal matters
Counselor (General)	1	General advisor
Deputy assistant to the president (Management)	12	Adviser to chief of staff, communications-production, communications-policy & planning, deputy to senior adviser, appointments and scheduling, advance, political affairs, public liaison, intergovernmental affairs, legislative affairs (2), Oval Office operations
Deputy assistant to the president (Special)	1	Chief of staff to the First Lady
Deputy assistant to the president (Policy)	3	National Security, Strategic Initiatives, Freedom Corps
Special assistant to the president (Management)	3	Media affairs, social secretary, cabinet liaison

Source: Compiled from data in *The United States Government Manual, 2005–2006* (Washington, DC: Government Printing Office, 2005), 86–87.

in polling and other forms of political communication have made these positions more specialized than in the past. After Republicans captured control of Congress in 1994, President Clinton turned for help to Dick Morris, a political consultant he had worked with in the past. Morris's role at first was a secret, even to other White House staff. Later, when his role was known, Morris was a controversial figure, judged by certain White House staff to be disruptive of their work.[7]

The position and influence of Karl Rove in the Bush 43 presidency was never covert. He was acknowledged to have been the principal political architect of Bush's campaigns for election and reelection. During the second term he was appointed deputy chief of staff in the WHO, a position with influence on policy as well as politics.

The Vice President

The president's first appointment in government comes before winning office. A running mate is chosen who then serves as vice president. For most of history, the principal job of the vice president historically was to be ready to assume the presidency in cases of the death, incapacity, removal, or resignation of the president. For many, the title might better have been "Vice Asterisk." Take a test: Who was FDR's first vice president? Woodrow Wilson's? (See the appendix for answers.) However, nine vice presidents became presidents, with five of these subsequently running for a full term of their own, four successfully.

Presidents do not plan to leave office involuntarily and therefore they have, in the past, typically selected running mates more to help them get elected than to help in governing later. Recent practice, however, has been to acknowledge the potential usefulness of a vice president once in office, often to strengthen a presidential weakness. For example, Carter had no Washington or congressional experience, and he chose a respected veteran senator, Walter Mondale, as his running mate. Lacking a background in foreign policy, Reagan chose an experienced diplomat, George H. W. Bush. Like Carter, Clinton and Bush 43 needed help on Capitol Hill and elsewhere in Washington. Clinton chose Al Gore, who had served in both the House of Representatives and Senate. Bush 43 selected Richard Cheney, whose service in the House of Representatives, the White House as Ford's chief of staff, and the cabinet as secretary of defense, made him one of the most broadly experienced vice presidents in history.

In each of these cases, the vice president aided the president in making connections to Congress and the bureaucracy. This greater role in governance has resulted in a larger and more articulated staff for the vice president, now greater in size than those for presidents in the immediate post–World War II era. Vice President Cheney's staff in 2005 included the following positions:

Fig. 5.2. President Reagan lunches with Vice President Bush, a regular occasion for consultation. (National Archives and Records Administration [ARC 198591])

Chief of Staff and Deputy Chief of Staff
Chief of Staff for Mrs. Cheney
Five Assistants to the Vice President
One each: Counsel, Principal Deputy Assistant for National
    Security, Press Secretary, Executive Assistant, Director
    of Correspondence
Two Deputy Assistants to the Vice President[8]

One consideration in promoting the active involvement of vice presidents is the extent of their own ambition to be president. It has become almost routine in the post–World War II era for vice presidents to run for the presidency. Excluding those who took over as presidents (Johnson and Ford), the list includes Nixon (1960), Humphrey (1968), Bush (1988), and Gore (2000). Mondale (1976) and Quayle (2000) ran after having served as vice president. Nixon ran a second time (1968), and Quayle did not win the nomination in 2000. Of these, only Bush 41 won as a sitting vice president, and Nixon won in his second effort.

Recognizing the unique relationship between the president and vice president, Harvard professor Richard E. Neustadt forwarded some "rules of thumb" to his former student, Al Gore, then running for vice president. Among the most relevant rules are these:

1. The VP reminds the P of his mortality; the P reminds the VP of his dependency.
2. The White House staff lives in the present, the VP's staff in the future.
3. The VP can't be fired, but the P can ignore, or haze him—and, if the P, then staff will too—with relative impunity.
4. The only thing more frustrating than being bypassed is to have one's advice heard, pondered, and not taken.[9]

The working relationships between recent presidents and vice presidents have been quite strong and productive. Most vice presidents in the future may be expected to have presidential ambitions. After all, they are in a superb position to observe and to reflect on how they might have managed a decision. However, the vice president with the most responsibilities in recent decades, Richard Cheney, announced well in advance that he had no intention of running for president.

The Presidential Branch

White House staff efforts to connect with the permanent government so as to coordinate policy and politics inevitably replicate functions performed elsewhere. The EOP requires experienced and expert staff familiar with government programs, suggesting the need for low turnover. The WHO, as the organization tailored more to an individual president, will also need its team of policy and operational functionaries. As was stated forcefully in *The Music Man*, they all "need to know the territory."

Nelson W. Polsby has observed that the institutionalization of this "help" to the president has produced a *presidential branch* "separate and apart from the executive branch."[10] What results is not exactly a chain of command, as in the military. Rather it is communication taking the form of focused coordination, that is, favoring the president's policy and political preferences.

This work by White House staff can lead to conflicts and interference with the efforts of the president's own appointees in the cabinet departments and other agencies, as well as the bureaucrats in those units. And, as with any expanding organization, competition may develop among staff for the boss's favor. George E. Reedy, who served President Johnson as press secretary, likened White House staff machinations to "the life of the barnyard, as set forth so graphically in the study of the pecking order among chickens."[11]

One need not accept Reedy's rather harsh and vivid portrayal to comprehend the hazards for presidents in insuring that this presidential branch work for them and not simply advance the ambitions of their staffs or get in the way of effective governance. It is unquestionably the case that working for the president can be an important credentialing experience, leading to other positions of status and financial reward if one moves to the private sector. In fact, Washington is teeming with former presidential staff appointees now lobbying for various interests. Thus presidents cannot always be assured that the goals of staff will mesh with those set for the administration.

Other management problems within the presidential branch include staff persons becoming public figures (something advised against in the 1937 report), preventing leaks as staff expands, maintaining personal loyalty among those less known to the president, and avoiding staff fatigue.

The latter point is less well recognized than the others. White House staff positions can easily become open-ended in two respects: working hours and job definition. Jeffrey H. Birnbaum, in his book *Madhouse*, an analysis of "the private turmoil of working for the president," states "the White House is a place for young people. Few others are able to survive its rigors."[12] The pace and lack of clear specification of responsibilities take their toll. As Birnbaum emphasizes, expectations of the president are greater than can possibly be met, yet the staff are responsible for meeting them.

Conclusion

The focus of this chapter has been on the connections to be made by new presidents with the government they are expected to lead. It has recounted developments contributing to the growing complexity and intensity of this task. Presidents and their advisers can study how it was done before. But no one president is like another and so much depends on the preferences, qualities, capabilities, resources, backgrounds, and goals that shape the style and approach of the new leader in town. Presidents are advised to "hit the ground running." Yet without having established reliable connections to the permanent government, a new president and staff may only be running in place.

White House operations do tend to improve with time. As it happens, however, just as the staff and major appointees are settling into governing routines, it is time for the president to seek reelection. Three things happen at that point: the inner circle becomes occupied with the campaign (staff are often added specifically for that purpose), those major appointees still serving think seriously about resigning their positions, and reelection itself alters how those in the permanent government view the White House—the so-called lame duck condition. Thus, presidents in their second term must make organizational adjustments just as their network of connections has matured. To say the least, connecting to and leading the government are dynamic processes requiring patience and deftness.

Notes

1. Gary Wills, quoted in Charles O. Jones, "The Presidency and the Press," *Journal of the Press and Politics*, vol. 1, no. 2 (1996): 16.
2. Peri E. Arnold, *Making the Managerial Presidency: Comprehensive Reorganization Planning, 1905–1980* (Princeton, NJ: Princeton University Press, 1986), 361–62.
3. President's Committee on Administrative Management, *Administrative Management of the Government of the United States* (Washington, DC: Government Printing Office, 1937), 5.
4. The Bureau of the Budget was originally created in 1921 by the Budget and Accounting Act. Originally a part of the Department of the Treasury, it was moved to the EOP with the Reorganization Act of 1939.
5. See *The United States Government Manual, 2005–2006* (Washington, DC: Government Printing Office, 2005), 92 for the full list.
6. For details, see Stephen Hess (with James P. Pfiffner), *Organizing the Presidency*, 3rd ed. (Washington, D.C., Brookings Institution Press, 2002), chs. 3–10.

7. For details see Dick Morris, *Behind the Oval Office: Winning the Presidency in the Nineties* (New York: Random House, 1997) and George Stephanopoulos, *All Too Human: A Political Education* (New York: Little, Brown, 1999).

8. *The United States Government Manual, 2005–2006* (Washington, DC: Government Printing Office, 2005), 88.

9. Charles O. Jones, ed., *Preparing To Be President: The Memos of Richard E. Neustadt* (Washington, DC: American Enterprise Institute Press, 2000), 131,

10. Nelson W. Polsby, "Some Landmarks in Presidential-Congressional Relations," in *Both Ends of the Avenue: The President, the Executive Branch, and the Congress,* ed. Anthony King (Washington, DC: American Enterprise Institute, 1983), 3.

11. George E. Reedy, *The Twilight of the Presidency* (New York and Cleveland: World Publishing Company, 1970), xiv.

12. Jeffrey H. Birnbaum, *Madhouse* (New York: Times Books, 1996), 244.

References

Arnold, Peri E. *Making the Managerial Presidency: Comprehensive Reorganization Planning, 1905–1996.* 2nd ed. Lawrence: University Press of Kansas, 1998.

Campbell, Colin. *Managing the Presidency: Carter, Reagan, and the Search for Executive Harmony.* Pittsburgh: University of Pittsburgh Press, 1986.

Hart, John. *The Presidential Branch: From Washington to Clinton.* 2nd ed. New York: Seven Bridges Press/Chatham House, 1995.

Hess, Stephen. *Organizing the Presidency.* 3rd ed. With James P. Pfiffner. Washington, DC: Brookings Institution Press, 2002.

Nelson, Michael L., ed. *Guide to the Presidency.* Vol. 2. *Congressional Quarterly,* 1996.

Patterson, Bradley H. Jr. *Ring of Power: Inside the West Wing and Beyond.* Washington, DC: Brookings Institution Press, 2000.

The United States Government Manual, 2005–2006. Washington, DC: Government Printing Office, 2005.

Chapter 6
Presidents at Work: Making Law and Doing Policy

Presidents are decision makers who work at a job structured by the tension between what is expected and what can be delivered. The strain derives mostly from the way the Founders sought to make a government that would work—but not too efficiently. So the Founders divvied up authority and constrained power. Consequently, making decisions is typically a joint enterprise. Congress can pass bills, but the president signs them into law. Presidents can negotiate treaties, but two thirds of the Senate must approve. The Supreme Court can negate a law, but Congress and the president can achieve their purposes by enacting a law that avoids the issue raised by the Court. I can't help but think that the Founders would be pleased with how the separated system has developed, most importantly because many of the same institutional issues that were debated in Philadelphia remain as core topics today, most notably in this context: How powerful ought the president to be?

Joint enterprise or no, presidents are held accountable for what happens in Washington. It is the president's job approval that is tested regularly, now hundreds of times a year. Why? There is but one president at a time. Presidents are, effectively, the only nationally elected officials. They serve as the commanders in chief, a title that surely conveys authority, and so they are expected to lead and achieve. No excuses, certainly not one that states: "But you don't understand, it is a joint enterprise."

Coincidentally, presidents are expected to observe the limits of their authority and status—to avoid abusing their authority, to acknowledge the legitimacy of the other branches, and to respect the right of people to know the what and how of decision making. Is it fair to hold presidents accountable for what happens in a shared-powers government? I leave that to you to decide. It is, however, clear from history that they will be held accountable for the reasons stated, and therefore it comes with the job. Those who seek the presidency surely know this in advance. Those who occupy the White House experience their preeminence in responsibility first hand. Leave it to President Truman to have stated it bluntly and tersely: "The buck stops here."

This chapter goes inside the president's working world to reveal the nature of making decisions in the national government, and the president's roles and functions in the processes involved. Interdependency is a major feature of an interlocking separation-of-powers system, with each branch exercising authority that enables the work of the others.

Lawmaking and its execution provide examples of interdependency. Presidents designate agendas and propose what should be done, Congresses represent constituency interests in legislating from this agenda, the bureaucracy implements the laws passed by congresses and signed by presidents, and the courts judge challenges to laws and how they are executed. It is true that the institutions share and compete for powers, but seldom will the work of one be mistaken for the work of another. Should there be encroachment, that interference will likely be criticized, perhaps even challenged in the courts.

Given their national and international exposure, presidents typically need to think prospectively, weighing the effects of initiatives and decisions on their capacities to govern in the future. George W. Bush was quoted as saying: "I think my job is to stay ahead of the moment. A president . . . can get so bogged down in the moment that you're unable to be the strategic thinker that you're supposed to be."[1] Richard E. Neustadt had a more nuanced analysis:

> My fundamental question [in thinking about the presidency] remains the same throughout, namely how to think about the possible effects of one's own choices on one's own prospects for personal influence within the institutional setting of a given office. . . . This amounts to seeking the essence of thinking politically, an endless search since that is so much an instinctive, intuitive process.[2]

For Neustadt, "the essence of thinking politically" guides presidents into protecting their influence for making future choices. For example, Clinton reduced his options in 1994 in regard to national health care proposals when he threatened to veto a version not to his liking. Speaking before Congress in the State of the Union Message, the president made his arguments for a health care plan. Then he waved his pen in the air and warned of a veto. The former president acknowledged the mistake in his memoirs:

> I thought my argument was effective except for one thing: at the end . . . I held up a pen and said I would use it to veto any bill that didn't guarantee health insurance to all Americans. . . . It was an unnecessary red flag to my opponents in Congress. Politics is about compromise and people expect Presidents to win, not posture for them.[3]

In the end, the plan failed in both houses of a Democratic Congress.

Working with Congress

Presidents interact with countless officials and groups in their manifold formal and informal roles, for example, as diplomats with foreign nations, as party leaders with politicians, as managers with agency personnel, as educators with the public, and as commanders with the armed forces. Among the most important and perpetual relationships, however, are those between the president and members of Congress. The budget process alone ensures that the president will pay close attention to Capitol Hill. "No Money shall be drawn from the Treasury but in Consequence of Appropriations made by Law." (Art. I, Sec. 9). Put simply: Lacking appropriations by Congress, the government is stymied, constitutionally unable to draw funds from the Treasury, as happened in 1995 when President Clinton and the Republican Congress were at loggerheads over the budget.

Presidents differ in their working relationships with Congress. Their political and governmental backgrounds largely explain this variation. A few examples illustrate the differences among recent presidents.

Lyndon Johnson served in the House (twelve years) and Senate (twelve years, ten as a leader). He was *majority leader* as president. "He learned early and never forgot the basic skill of the politician, the ability to divide any number by two and add one."[4] As was the case when he was in Congress, Johnson was a master at building majorities on Capitol Hill in support of Great Society programs.

Richard Nixon also served in Congress but not as a leader and for six, not twenty-four, years. His interest and expertise were in foreign policy. He was *foreign minister* as president, preferring to work on national security and international relations issues. As such, he did not want frequent contact with members of Congress whose primary interests tend to be in domestic issues. A House

Republican was quoted as saying: "I pretty well concluded that there was almost no way to contact him except if you had a personal relationship."[5]

Jimmy Carter did not invite genuine contact with Congress either. The reasons were different, however, again related to his background. Elected as a post-Watergate president, Carter was skeptical of the politics of compromise that dominated Congress. He was the *political layman* as president. Ignoring his narrow win in 1976, it was his view that the president represents all the people and has the resources to develop comprehensive programs. He stressed the importance of doing the right thing over bargaining.

Reagan, Clinton, and Bush 43 were, like Carter, governors before serving as presidents. Accordingly they brought variations of an executive orientation to their work with Congress. True to his profession in private life, Reagan was an *actor* as president. His view of his status was best summarized by the subtitle of Lou Cannon's book: *President Reagan: The Role of a Lifetime*. Unlike Carter, Reagan was not in the least opposed to compromise, which fit his understanding of the role to be played by the president. He viewed his responsibilities as those of designating and defining a limited agenda, delegating responsibility to staff for working out details, agreeing to a reasonable compromise, and declaring victory. In his political theater, he endorsed Clinton's view that "people expect presidents to win."

Clinton was a *campaigner* as president. Few presidents in history had as much experience in running for office—for the House of Representatives, for attorney general and six times for governor in Arkansas, and twice for president. He continued to sell his programs even after winning the presidency. Each State of the Union Message was followed by travel to bolster public support for his proposals. He was more broadly ambitious in proposing legislation than was Reagan, who concentrated on a few big-ticket items.

Bush 43 adopted Clinton's practice of campaigning for policy as well as election. In fact, Bush topped Clinton's record-setting travel, prompting one scholar to dub Bush as a campaigner president.[6] Clinton's and Bush's styles and purposes differed, however. Bush 43's way of working has been that of a *pure executive* as president. He is among the most separationist of presidents, believing that the president and Congress have distinctive functions. He has viewed his job as that of designating the issues and offering proposals to Congress, much less to work Johnson-like to build majorities on Capitol Hill. His campaigning has primarily been to convince the public that he has the right priorities and the most effective plans. As with Nixon, he also has demonstrated an expansive interpretation of his powers in regard to national security issues.

Other post–World War II presidents show equally diverse manners of dealing with Congress: Eisenhower—*military commander*; Kennedy—*junior senator*; Ford—*minority leader*;

Fig. 6.1. The contemporary president on the road. George W. Bush campaigns for support. (U.S. Air Force photo by Staff Sgt. Jim Verchio)

Bush 41—*career diplomat.* Presidents approach the job with individual perspectives that help shape their responses to the issues that they encounter and to the events that generate those issues.

Types and Settings of Power

Presidents make many types of decisions in varieties of settings. Their policy world is fast paced and complex. They deal in policy substance and its phases, processes, and interactive effects. Much of what happens is routine, essentially handled by the bureaucrats, appointed political executives and their aides, and policy specialists, presumably all attentive to presidential priorities. Ultimately, however, presidents are held responsible because they have the authority to say yes, no, or try again.

Policy Substance

Substance refers to the "what" of policy, that is, the meat of what is being considered. The range is enormous, but most issues fit within two broad categories: domestic and foreign. The two sets have interactive effects. Energy supply and demand is a fine example of a domestic issue with enormous impact on foreign policy, and vice versa. Yet each set retains enough distinctive features to justify the categories. Among these is the greater role played by Congress in domestic over foreign and national security issues. Thus, the president's role differs markedly between the two sets, having substantially more discretion in foreign affairs.

The range of substantive domestic matters is illustrated in table 6.1. Provided are the major pieces of domestic legislation enacted during Clinton's two-term presidency (1993–2001) and the first term of Bush 43 (2001–05). The laws are grouped by whether the president's party had majorities in Congress (same party or split party). First, take note that the short titles of the major laws listed in table 6.1 reveal an impressive range of topics: fiscal, social

Table 6.1 Major Domestic Legislation, 1993–2005

Clinton (1993–2001)

Same Party	Opposite Party
103rd Congress (9 cases): Deficit reduction, Voter registration, Americorps, Student loans, Education, Crime, Desert protection, Abortion clinics	104th Congress (14 cases): State mandates, Congress accounting, Lobbying, Lawsuits, Welfare, Telecommunications, Agriculture, Line-item veto, Spending cuts, Health insurance, Minimum wage, Pesticides, Safe water, Immigration
	105th Congress (7 cases): Balanced budget, FDA overhaul, Adoption, Transportation, IRS overhaul, Public housing, Teachers
	106th Congress (5 cases): Banking, Y2K plan, Education, Everglades, Community renewal

Bush (2001–05)

Same Party	Split Party*
107th Congress (1 case): Tax cuts 108th Congress (8 cases): Prescription drugs, Tax cuts, Partial birth abortion, Forests, Corporate tax, Disaster relief, Unborn victims	107th Congress (10 cases): Airline bailout, Airline security, Emergency spending, Education, DHS created, Campaign finance, Agriculture, Corporate reform, Election reform, Terrorism insurance

*Refers to Democratic majority in the Senate, Republican majority in the House. For the first five months, Republicans had a Senate majority.

Source: Compiled from David R. Mayhew, *Divided We Govern: Party Control, Lawmaking, and Investigations, 1946–2002* (New Haven, CT: Yale University Press, 2005), 208–13, and http://pantheon.yale.edu/~dmayhew.

welfare, environment, crime, health care, elections, lobbying, institutions, reorganization, domestic security, business, agriculture, and disaster. Each of these matters has an institutional home in the bureaucratic agencies and the congressional committees. These units attend to the clienteles affected by legislation, and those clienteles will lobby the president and Congress to acknowledge and support their views. One can hardly expect otherwise in a representative democracy, but it does complicate the task of proposing and instituting change where those benefiting from a government program want to keep what they have.

Second, observe that major laws get enacted whether or not the president's party has majorities on Capitol Hill. *In fact, there was no significant difference in the average number of major laws passed whether a Congress was of the same or opposite party as that of the president.* The 103rd and 108th congresses had presidential-party majorities, with an average of 8.5 laws passed, very nearly the same as the average of nine laws for the four split-party congresses. An additional major law was passed in the few months of the 107th Congress when the Republicans had a narrow majority in the Senate. It is apparent that gridlock is not inevitable when the parties split control of the branches.

Third, table 6.1 shows how nimble a president must be in accommodating shifting party fortunes. There were four changes in party control in the twelve years of Clinton's two terms and Bush's first term: from same party in the 103rd Congress to opposite party in the 104th, 105th, and 106th, back to same party briefly in the 107th, then to split party (Senate only) for the rest of the 107th, and finally a return to same party in the 108th. Different strategies are required for these different party arrangements. Presidents lose their dominance in designating the agenda if the other party is in the majority on Capitol Hill. And whereas party unity will win the day when the president's party

117

has a majority, they need votes from the other side if the opposition party is in charge.

Presidents have greater independence in shaping and implementing foreign and national security policy. The constitutional status of commander in chief, along with treaty making authority and ambassadorial appointments, provide prerogatives to reinforce the president's role as national leader. Table 6.2 shows that many fewer major laws or resolutions are purely foreign or national security policy. Of the fourteen listed for Clinton and Bush 43, four involved trade agreements, another seven involved terrorism and the Iraq war, all but one occurring in the Bush presidency. Several of these cases had important domestic implications, notably the trade agreements, intelligence gathering, and the

Table 6.2 Major Foreign and National Security Legislation, 1993–2005

Clinton (1993–2001)	
Same Party	**Opposite Party**
103rd Congress (2 cases): NAFTA, GATT	104th Congress (1 case): Antiterrorism
	105th Congress (2 cases): Chemical weapons, NATO expansion
	106th Congress (1 case): Permanent trading w/China

Bush (2001–05)	
Same Party	**Split Party***
108th Congress (3 cases): AIDS funding, Defense spending, intelligence reform	107th Congress (5 cases): Use of force (Afghanistan), Patriot act, Iraq resolution, Fast-track trade authority, 9/11 commission

*See table 6.1.

Source: See table 6.1

Patriot Act that provided greater powers for the Department of Justice in combating terrorism.

The president's discretionary powers in foreign and national security policy are substantial and well illustrated by the Clinton and Bush 43 presidencies. These powers may become the subject of controversy, often inviting congressional investigations and oversight largely because Congress had little or no role in the initiatives taken by the president.

Outstanding examples of discretionary actions during the Clinton presidency include military action and peace initiatives. Congress was not asked to authorize any of these actions. A bombing campaign against Bosnian Serbs was initiated in late August 1995 by NATO, with U.S. participation authorized by Clinton. Clinton ordered the bombing of Baghdad in early September 1996, following attacks on a Kurdish-controlled city, and again in December 1998, with the failure of Iraq to cooperate with United Nations' inspectors. An air war against Serbia was launched in March 1999, forcing the Yugoslav president to withdraw troops from Kosovo.

Clinton also sponsored peace initiatives as largely executive actions. In November 1995, the "Dayton Peace Accords" ended the conflict in Bosnia, and U.S. troops were sent to keep the peace. In July 2000 Clinton hosted a summit at Camp David to resolve issues between Israel and Palestine. He was also personally active in resolving the disputes in Northern Ireland.

Likewise, the Bush 43 presidency provides countless examples of the president making military and diplomatic commitments with little or no direct involvement of Congress. Even the congressional 2001 Use of Force (Afghanistan) and 2002 Iraq resolutions largely left open the timing, rationale, and form of military action. Much of the controversy that developed over treatment of prisoners resulted from executive and military decisions regarding the incarceration of terrorists, decisions that in the earliest stages were not subject to the kind of close scrutiny that follows from open congressional hearings. Similarly, questions were raised in 2006 about warrantless surveillance by the National Security Agency of suspected terrorists' communications to persons in the United States, a practice ordered by the president and later the subject of court review.

President Bush was initially reluctant to be involved in resolving Israeli-Palestinian issues. Later, however, his administration became heavily committed with the "Road Map to Peace" initiative in May 2003 and in working through the United Nations to fashion a cease-fire agreement when war broke out between Israel and Hezbollah, operating from Lebanon, in the summer of 2006. The nuclear threat posed by developments in North Korea was met with diplomatic efforts, working through countries in the region (notably China, Japan, Russia, and South Korea). Diplomacy too was relied on early in seeking to curb Iran's nuclear ambitions, this time with European nations taking the lead. These are but a few examples to show that diplomacy is, and must be, primarily the province of the executive, with the president leading the way.

When purely executive actions produce positive results, support follows in Congress. When serious problems develop or the resolution of an issue takes longer than expected (as with the Vietnam War and the Iraq insurgency), congressional criticism mounts, investigations are initiated, and restrictions on the president's discretion are threatened or imposed.

But Congress is constrained if military action is underway. It has the power of the purse, but members are reluctant to deny funds to the troops. It is also the case in modern warfare that a military mission may have been completed by the time Congress acts. The problem is somewhat different in regard to diplomacy. Treaties require Senate approval (two-thirds of those present) and financial commitments need congressional authorization and appropriation. However the executive decides where, when, and what to negotiate. Congress does not have a separate diplomatic corps. In foreign policy, presidents exercise their greatest influence, whether Congress approves or not.

Policy Type

The president's role also differs by the type of policy under consideration. Most decisions fall into four broad categories: fresh initiatives, incremental adjustments in existing programs, major reforms to those programs on the books, and crisis response. Different types of policies lend themselves to more or less empowerment for the president.

Fresh initiatives are most likely to come from the executive and are often proposed when a new president takes office. For example, in his first year Clinton successfully proposed an Americorps to encourage young people to do volunteer work in the community in exchange for educational support. Bush 43 favored a faith-based initiative for spurring community-level aid to the disadvantaged. Congress did not enact the proposed legislation and so Bush issued an executive order initiating certain aspects of the proposal.

Fresh programs are more difficult to enact than in the past, in large part because of the cost of those put on the books in the Roosevelt through the Johnson presidencies. Entitlement programs such as Social Security, Medicare and Medicaid, federal aid to education, home loan guarantees, food stamps, and other welfare benefits, along with national defense, have left little room in the budget for new initiatives. Therefore new programs typically must include innovative financing, sometimes with proposals to reduce expenditures elsewhere.

Incrementalism characterizes most existing government programs for several reasons: more persons are covered by the benefits with growth and aging of the population, costs of living rise, and organized groups make claims. For example, the many programs providing benefits for senior citizens have grown in size as people live longer, have more health problems, and are represented by politically active groups, notably the American Association of Retired Persons (AARP).

The politics of incrementalism are predictable. Once in place, an entitlement program grows automatically. The only way to curb spending is to change the eligibility, a move most presidents and members of Congress are cautious in proposing. As the agenda designators, presidents learn that any such proposals, even for needed reforms, can ignite political firestorms on Capitol Hill and among beneficiaries. Presidents thus must carefully calculate the political risks involved in proposing major changes.

Major reforms of existing programs are occasionally proposed in spite of the political costs for taking a chance. There comes a time when most government programs are subject to serious review and change. That time will occur in the decades following the enactment of large-scale programs like those of Roosevelt's New Deal and Johnson's Great Society. Thus it is not surprising in recent years to find that the executive branch proposals to Congress have "reform" in their titles: for example, Social Security and welfare reform, Medicare reform, farm subsidy reform, public housing reform. Most often the changes that are proposed are by way of refinements, but occasionally they are root-and-branch reformulations, as with welfare reform in 1996, and generate intense controversy.

Those reforms proposed for Social Security are at a very high risk, as was confirmed for Bush 43 in 2005 when he supported private accounts as an option for a portion of payroll taxes paid. His plan did not get beyond the committee stage in either house of Congress. President Reagan also learned of the political costs when he suggested major changes in 1981, and Republicans had a net loss of twenty-five House seats in 1982. Immigration reform is

Fig. 6.2. President Roosevelt signs Social Security Act of 1935, a New Deal program. (Social Security Administration History Archives)

Fig. 6.3. President Johnson signs Medical Care for the Aged Act of 1965, a Great Society program, in the presence of former President Truman. (LBJ Library photo by Yoichi R. Okamoto [A985-6a])

also a political minefield, again as experienced by Bush 43 in 2006. Just the issue of how millions of illegal aliens should be treated is fraught with political risks.

It was long thought that welfare reform carried many of the same risks. President Clinton made it a priority in his first term, an unusual step for a Democrat. Yet he placed it second to health care reform, which was defeated. Meanwhile, congressional Republicans agreed with the welfare reform priority. When they gained majorities in the House and Senate in 1994, they took the initiative in fashioning a plan. President Clinton twice vetoed the bill but signed it when the Republican Congress passed it a third time. Many Democrats were critical of Clinton's action, some in his own administration resigned.

The risks for Clinton in these two cases—national health care and welfare reform—were multiple and sequential. He proposed taking on two major reforms, failed utterly in the first, then lost the initiative for the second, welfare reform, to the Republicans. Finally signing the Republican bill third time around invited criticism from his own party. There are few better cases of the hazards of proposing root-and-branch reforms.

Crisis response is of a different nature from the preceding policy types. By definition it is extraordinary, an interference with the regular order. Expectations are that response will come immediately from the executive, led and directed by the president. Congress will participate too but typically following the lead of the commander in chief. Presidents will then be judged by how effective they are in their responses.

The most recent example of crisis response is among the most dramatic in history: Bush 43's decisions following the terrorists' attacks on the World Trade Center in New York City and the Pentagon in Washington on September 11, 2001. The existing agenda of conventional domestic reforms was displaced by a host of homeland security and national defense issues. The partisanship of a narrowly split Congress and voting public shifted quickly to bipartisan support for President Bush's leadership. His job approval ratings soared to record heights and remained at high levels for the longest period of any president for the period in which these measures have been taken.

In striking contrast, support for the president was substantially less forthcoming for the war in Iraq, both initially and even more with continued insurgent attacks following the completion of full-scale military action. The difference? The president had difficulty persuading his critics and, eventually, many in the public that Saddam Hussein's rule in Iraq represented a crisis or that it was directly related to the war on terrorism. These doubts were reinforced by the failure to find weapons of mass destruction. In other words, the war in Iraq was not judged either by the public or many in Congress to be crisis response.

The Katrina hurricane was another example of crisis response, one substantially less favorable to the leadership of Bush 43 than 9/11. No one doubted that it was a crisis or that response was required by the national government. But the effects were regional, not national, and the offender was Mother Nature, not terrorists. True, 9/11 was also localized, but the threat was pervasive.

In the case of Katrina, coordination among federal, state, and local governments was inadequate to manage an exceptional natural disaster. The president was bound to bear the responsibility as the chief of the branch that was expected to react effectively. The Katrina disaster is a prime example of presidential responsibility whether or not public expectations are realistic in regard to his or the government's capacity to cope. It simply goes with the job of being at the top. No excuses.

Policy Process

The process by which policy is set in place and implemented can be broken down into several phases or functions: problem definition, agenda designation, option formulation, and program legitimation, implementation, and evaluation. The president and his aides play different roles in each of these phases, as do the other branches: bureaucratic, legislative, and judicial. Politics primarily determines presidential participation, its rationale and form. Still, it will become obvious that the president and executive branch perform especially vital functions in the early phases, given that it takes an organized and hierarchical structure to come up with priorities and proposals.

Problem definition starts it all. What requires the attention of the national government and why? There are, at minimum, two dimensions to consider: the broad issue (e.g., terrorism) and the specific problems (e.g., homeland security, identifying and capturing or eradicating the terrorists, managing the social and economic effects). Presidents ordinarily play a key role in identifying and articulating the issues and defining the problems to be dealt with. They are in a strong position to direct public attention to an issue.

Yet presidents do not have the last word. What requires attention and why is often the subject of debate in Congress and the media, even where there is broad agreement on the seriousness of the issue. For example, in a post-9/11 America, immigration was generally acknowledged to be a vital issue. But some policy makers defined the problem as failure to control the borders and enforce existing laws; others emphasized the need to cope with millions of illegal immigrants who have become a significant force in the American economy as a source of labor.

Will presidents be held responsible even if their preferences are modified by changes made in the lawmaking process? Absolutely.

That even holds for presidents who opposed what was put in place originally (for example, Reagan for any number of government programs he opposed).

Agenda designation is essentially a priority-setting exercise. It is a supremely political act, and presidents have significant constitutional, institutional, and electoral advantages for specifying priorities. They deliver the State of the Union message, they are served by an elaborate bureaucracy that can supply detailed justifications for priorities, and they work closely with budget makers who know the fiscal record and effects of priorities being set.

Presidents differ in the extent to which they capitalize on these advantages. Determinants include the president's philosophy of governing (more activist or more passive), the nature and number of major issues, and the strength of the opposition party. For example, Eisenhower was not a strong policy activist; he served during relatively calm times, with few major issues; and Democrats had majorities in both houses of Congress during six of his eight years as president. By contrast, Johnson brought an expansionist outlook to his presidency, he had to manage an increasingly unpopular war in Vietnam, and his party had huge congressional majorities.

As expected, given the three determinants (philosophy, issues, and strength of the opposition), there are several combinations among the post–World War II presidents. Reagan had a philosophy of limited government, seeking to reduce taxes and bureaucracy; served during a period of relative calm; and had the surprise advantage of a Republican Senate for six of his eight years in office. His agenda dominated policy politics during his first years in office, and his legislative success in cutting taxes influenced the agendas of those presidents to follow.

Clinton and Bush 43 are interesting cases. The first began with an ambitious perspective on government's role, later modified; faced

127

few domestic or foreign crises; and soon lost Democratic majorities in Congress. Congressional Republicans, mostly in the person of Speaker of the House Newt Gingrich, took charge of agenda designation in 1995, later to see Clinton's dominance restored after his reelection in 1996. Bush 43 campaigned in 2000 on a "compassionate conservatism" agenda of moderate to conservative priorities. Hardly under way in pursuing these priorities, he observed the transformation of relative calm into escalating crises from 9/11 forward. He worked consistently with very narrow Republican margins in Congress (even losing a Republican Senate majority in 2001 for eighteen months), a condition that promoted intense partisanship in acting on his priorities.

A president with limited political capital can expect others to assume the role of agenda designator. House Speakers James Wright (D-Texas) and Newt Gingrich (R-Georgia) were active agenda-setters when Bush 41 and Clinton experienced weak political status on Capitol Hill in 1989 and 1995 respectively. And when Democrats became a majority in the Senate in 2001 they were in a position to designate the agenda for that chamber, one very different from that preferred by Bush 43. Even more dramatic for Bush 43 was the Democratic takeover of both houses of Congress in the 2006 midterm election. Agenda designation required consultation with opposition party leaders.

Option formulation too is a natural function of the executive, due primarily to the expertise represented in the bureaucracy and its hierarchical structure. Presidents and their staffs make promises in campaigns and in response to issues during their service in the White House. Usually these pledges lack a detailed plan. Rather they require development by specialists within the relevant cabinet department or agency. Likewise, congressional committee staffs, often working with the personal staffs of the members, prepare modifications or alternatives.

Rarely can presidents expect that Congress will endorse their options in full, even when their party has large majorities in that branch. Johnson's Medicare proposal in 1965 was modified substantially by the Democratic Chair of the House Committee on Ways and Means, Wilbur Mills (D-Arkansas). Staying with a health care example, Clinton had his proposal for national reform rejected in both houses in spite of Democratic majorities. Efforts by House and Senate Democrats to design alternatives also faltered.

Still for the major issues it is typically the president who says: "Let's start here with this." Every top-level bureaucrat and member of Congress has a drawer (or more likely a hard drive these days) full of options. None has the cachet of presidents, however, or the audience for publicizing their options.

Legitimation is the process by which an option, usually a compromise, is approved. Mostly this is a legislative function, though presidents and their staffs are actively involved as bills move forward. Majority support is garnered through a sequence of stages within committees, the House and Senate chambers, and conferences between the two chambers. This process may take months, even years. It is not uncommon with certain controversial proposals for Congress to repeat the stages several times before attaining agreements in all of the venues required for final passage. Because of the filibuster in the Senate, it may require a super majority (60 percent) to pass a bill in that chamber. And by constitutional provision a two-thirds Senate majority is required for treaties and a two-thirds majority in both chambers for a constitutional amendment or to override a presidential veto.

Presidents, their aides, and department and agency personnel are typically active in this majority-building enterprise—sometimes in support, other times in opposition. A change in presidents, which ordinarily means a change in party, can mean a reversal in White

House support or opposition. Ultimately the president has the constitutional authority to sign or veto a bill, or to let it become law without his signature after a ten-day period, Sundays excluded (unless Congress has adjourned, in which case it will not become law) (Art. I, Sec. 7). Presidents frequently use this vital authority of saying "yes" or "no" to influence lawmaking during the several stages of majority building, for example by threatening to veto a bill unless changes are made or withdrawing support, with the potential effect of changing votes.

There is a tendency to keep score in lawmaking by counting the bills passed and signed into law in a session of Congress. But progress may be slow on major national issues because difficult issues have to be resolved. Scoring failure to pass as a loss often masks progress being made on such matters. For example, it took some thirty years for the federal government to enact an aid to education program, long an exclusive province of state and local governments. Racial, religious, and federalism issues had to be resolved before a bill could finally gain majority support in both houses. Bills would pass in the House, only then to be filibustered by southern Democrats in the Senate. The Elementary and Secondary Education Act eventually passed in 1965 as part of Johnson's "Great Society" program.

Crisis can often speed up the legitimation process. Following 9/11, Congress passed the Patriot Act, a sweeping measure to provide the attorney general with authority for gathering intelligence on terrorists (wiretaps, searches, detention, other means of surveillance). Committee hearings and votes were bypassed in the Senate, and the Speaker intervened in the House to send a bill favored by the administration to the floor. The final bill passed overwhelmingly in both houses. Four years later it took months to pass a reauthorization of the Patriot Act.

Implementation is fundamentally a bureaucratic function, for which the president as chief executive will be held responsible.

Lawmakers will typically provide directions on how and where programs are to be implemented. But bureaucrats are in charge of the applications, often with substantial discretion, depending on how much Congress instructs them. State and local governments often play a major role in implementing domestic programs, an additional complication in designating responsibility.

Large-scale programs that represent new ventures, reorganizations, or major shifts in policy may take years to implement effectively. Medicare and Medicaid, enacted in 1965, are prime examples of substantial national government interventions into a multifaceted, semipublic health care system, one lacking synchronization. What began as relatively modest programs in the 1960s now are measured in hundreds of billions of dollars. In 2004 a prescription drug benefit was added, again accompanied in the early months by serious implementation difficulties.

Implementation of a different sort characterizes the federal government's response to calamities. Disaster relief programs have been expanded in recent decades. Almost by definition, however, it is hard to prepare for the unanticipated. Hurricane Katrina along the Gulf Coast in 2005 was such an occurrence, arguably the greatest natural disaster ever in the United States. Government response was judged to be inadequate for many reasons: the magnitude of the disaster, a major reorganization of crisis response agencies underway at all three levels of government, breakdown of communications and law enforcement, lack of coordination among state and local agencies, and uncertainties about who was in charge of what. Yet the responsibility for these and other failings was judged to be that of President Bush, an opinion held by most officials, the general public, and, ultimately, the president himself. The Katrina experience is a classic case of presidential accountability regardless of the circumstances. Among other purposes served is that of placing responsibility with the official in the best position to make change.

Evaluation is the most diversified of the policy activities. Every branch is involved, along with private interests and organizations. The executive agencies charged with implementing programs typically must report to Congress on their progress in achieving goals. Inspector generals within these agencies have the responsibility of investigating fraud and misconduct. The Office of Management and Budget (OMB) evaluates programs on a continuous basis as it prepares budgets. White House staff are ever attentive to the effectiveness of programs, especially those associated with the president's policy preferences. And presidential commissions are frequently appointed to evaluate a program and make recommendations for change.

Congressional committees have the responsibility of overseeing the implementation of programs. This oversight may occur in several forms: as a routine exercise in reauthorization and appropriation; through investigations, either by authorizing committees or the two oversight committees (Oversight and Government Reform in the House, Homeland Security and Governmental Affairs in the Senate); or by the work of the Government Accountability Office (GAO). The latter is a legislative branch agency specifically charged to provide Congress with information about the effectiveness of government programs.

The judicial branch, too, may be asked to evaluate a program, testing it against a constitutional standard. Judicial review is not specifically assigned to the courts in Article III, but Chief Justice John Marshall argued successfully that it was emphatically implied in the Constitution, even in the oath taken by judges (*Marbury v. Madison*, 1803). A case is, however, required for the courts to exercise this authority. They cannot routinely apply a constitutional standard to laws as they are passed by Congress and signed by the president.

Last, clientele groups, the media, think tanks, public interest or watchdog groups, task forces, and candidate organizations continuously evaluate programs on the books. The media play an especially important role for two reasons: their adversarial role in regard to politics and government, and the quantum increase in media outlets in recent decades. The first is explained by what is typically judged to be news—that which is negative more than positive. The second represents a phase change in communication. Not only are there new forms due to electronic developments but, as well, coverage is constant, "24/7" as the phrase has it. One consequence is White House adaptation by greatly expanding its communications operations. What was once a press secretary with a small staff is now several assistants to the president for communication-related functions, including speechwriting, community outreach, advance work for presidential travel, communications in regard to policy and planning, public liaison, and intergovernmental affairs.

Policy Coordination: Budgeting

For decades presidents dominated budgeting. The Budget and Accounting Act of 1921 authorized the president to prepare an annual budget, assisted by a Bureau of the Budget (originally a part of the Department of Treasury, later a part of the Executive Office of the President and still later renamed the Office of Management and Budget—OMB). "The [1921] act . . . marks one of the most important changes in the balance of power between the branches of government in the nation's history."[7] The development of a budget in the executive is a multistage, year-long process of negotiation and refinement between the president and the departments and agencies, with OMB acting as the go-between. As shown in figure 6.1, the result is then sent to Congress in a budget message. In the past, the revenue, appropriations, and authorizing committees in Congress relied almost entirely on the president's budget in doing their work, without ever considering the plan as a whole.

In 1974 that all changed. Congress created its own budget process with the passage of the Congressional Budget and Impoundment Control Act. The act created House and Senate

The Budget Process

Executive Phases

Preparation (March → February): Year-long process of refinement and negotiation between the president, Office of Management and Budget (OMB), and agencies. OMB communicates presidential preferences and manages the details of adjusting agency requests to those preferences.

Submission (January → February): President's budget message prepared and budget submitted to Congress.

Update (July): President provides mid-session review.

Congressional Phases

Preparation (January → April): Three-month-long process of review and breakdown of current and president's budget involving the Congressional Budget Office (CBO), the Budget committees, and the revenue, appropriations, and authorizing committees.

Resolution (April): Congress passes a concurrent budget resolution, with guidelines for committees.

Reconciliation (June → September): Process of making adjustments to suit budget goals, again involving CBO, Budget Committees, and the revenue, appropriations, and authorizing committees.

Bureaucratic Phase

Execution (October 1 → September 30): Agencies implement programs as authorized and appropriated by Congress.

Fig 6.4. The Budget Process. (Compiled by the author from various sources)

budget committees, to be assisted by a Congressional Budget Office (CBO), and formalized a process for regulating and monitoring the work of the other committees. Deadlines were set to keep the process on schedule. Those deadlines have seldom been met.

Figure 6.4 shows an oversimplified display of how the process is *supposed* to work. As shown, each branch prepares a budget, although that in Congress is oriented to what has been prepared by the executive branch. The congressional process features negotiations between the budget committees in each house and the revenue, appropriations, and authorizing committees, with CBO providing expertise throughout. Not surprisingly, this process is tense and contestable, representing as it does the interests served by the various committees as well as their protections of jurisdictions. Yet in many ways it mirrors what happens in the executive between the agencies and the president and OMB.

One may also expect fights between the White House and Congress, none more intense in recent years than that in 1995 between President Clinton and congressional Republicans. Having won full control of Congress for the first time in forty years, Republicans were intent on winning the budget battle. Twice in the fall, 1995, they passed continuing resolutions cutting federal programs. President Clinton vetoed each one, twice resulting in partial shutdowns of the federal government. An agreement was finally reached in January 1996, more than three months beyond the start of the fiscal year (October 1, 1995). It was generally conceded that the president had won the political struggle. He had successfully stood down the Republican majorities on Capitol Hill. "A process ridden with partisanship, confrontation, and political gamesmanship ended in a stalemate [and] the Republicans finally gave up."[8] The consequence was that President Clinton had taken a major step in restoring what had been lost in 1994, his preeminence in designating the agenda.

The period after 1974 has featured split-party government and narrow margins as political context for making budgets. Only Presidents Carter (four years, 1977–81) and Clinton (1993–95) had comfortable party margins in Congress. Other presidents during this time (Ford, Reagan, Bush 41, Clinton after 1994, and Bush 43) either faced opposition party congresses (one house or both) or worked with very narrow party margins. While clashes were a certainty, presidents have the advantages of more detailed preparations, the veto threat, and a more coordinated approach to budgeting. They typically win more budget battles than they lose.[9]

Results in the Postwar Era

Earlier it was stated that not all presidents are created equal. Likewise, not all presidents produce equally. Events appear to make the difference. Some presidents preside at turning points in history, others govern in periods of relative calm. The difference is not necessarily in the qualities or abilities of the incumbent. Crises are not selective. Rather they test whoever happens to be in the White House at the time. And history shows that presidents who serve during crises are notable, typically ranked higher by historians and the public.

Post–World War II presidents at turning points include Truman, Johnson, Reagan, and Bush 43. Truman had to manage the end of World War II, cope with its aftermath, and deal with the Korean conflict. In addition, he took over for FDR, a president of great domestic and international achievements. Johnson, too, served out the term of a popular president, Kennedy, whose assassination insured support for his legacy. Johnson took charge of his predecessor's agenda and enacted the Great Society programs that would dominate domestic policy from that time forward. Johnson did significantly less well with the developing crisis in Vietnam, where his record was as unimpressive as it was imposing on domestic issues.

Economic circumstances in 1980 provided Reagan with the support to reduce taxes and shift resources to defense. The effect of the first was to alter policy debate as deficits mounted; the second eventually led to the end of the Cold War and, later, the collapse of the Soviet Union. And while it is early at this writing to judge Bush 43, few can doubt the significance of 9/11 as a historic event of major impact on policy and politics. The war on terrorism, as extended by Bush to the war in Iraq, has had a profound effect on foreign and domestic politics.

Events have also had an impact on the other postwar presidencies (Eisenhower, Nixon, Ford, Carter, Bush 41, and Clinton). None, however, matches the postwar rebuilding facing Truman, preserving the legacy of an assassinated president for Johnson, the opportunities for economic and government reform for Reagan, and the domestic and international threats posed by 9/11 in 2001 and beyond. Thus the terms in office of this second set of six presidents have been characterized more by efforts to consolidate, strengthen, and reform policies and programs already in place. Their presidencies were custodial, without implying anything disapproving about their personal abilities to cope with large-scale events had they occurred.

The remaining president in the postwar period, Kennedy, averted a potentially serious crisis with the threat posed by Soviet missiles in Cuba. Unquestionably his resolve in this matter was noteworthy and has been so acknowledged by historians. The problem in classifying Kennedy lies in the brevity of his service.

Conclusion

Government has a momentum independent of who happens to be in the White House. Presidents at work aid in maintaining this momentum, facilitating ordinary change, and responding to unanticipated events. They are enablers of lawmaking, policy making, and decision making. The executive branch is structured to promote these purposes in such a manner as to insure congressional reliance on the president.

Perhaps most striking about a president's work is the need for agility and adaptability. Presidents are expected to produce comprehensive and coordinated programs, yet by its nature, a separation of powers government allows for participation by others in many venues. As shown in this chapter, presidents have variable influence on policy substance (more on foreign and defense than domestic), policy type (most on crisis response), policy process (most on the early phases of problem definition, agenda designation, and option formulation), and policy coordination (a substantial degree on budgeting, though less than in the past). Finally, the work of presidents has the greatest historical impact as a consequence of unanticipated events that suspend the usual functioning of the separated system. These happenings, typically as crises, come to be the tests of leadership.

Notes

1. Quoted in Bob Woodward, *Bush at War* (New York: Simon and Schuster, 2002), 136.
2. Quoted in Charles O. Jones, "Richard E. Neustadt: Public Servant as Scholar," *Annual Review of Political Science* 6 (2003): 11.
3. Bill Clinton, *My Life* (New York: Alfred A. Knopf, 2004), 577.
4. Ralph K. Huitt, "Democratic Leadership in the Senate," *American Political Science Review* 55 (June, 1961): 337.
5. Quoted in Stephen J. Wayne, *The Legislative Presidency* (New York: Harper and Row, 1978), 161.
6. George C. Edwards, III, *Campaigning by Governing: The Politics of the Bush Presidency* (Upper Saddle River, NJ: Pearson Longman, 2006).
7. Donald F. Kettl, *Deficit Politics* (New York: Macmillan, 1992), 128.
8. Daniel J. Palazzolo, *Done Deal? The Politics of the 1997 Budget Agreement* (New York: Seven Bridges Press/Chatham House, 1999), 36.
9. An exception would be in 1990 when Bush 41 reneged on his "no new taxes" pledge. See Palazzolo, 33.

References

Greenstein, Fred I., ed. *Leadership in the Modern Presidency*. Cambridge, MA: Harvard University Press, 1988.
Hargrove, Erwin C., and Michael Nelson. *Presidents, Politics, and Policy*. Baltimore, MD: Johns Hopkins University Press, 1984.

Herring, E. Pendleton. *Presidential Leadership*. New York: Rinehart and Company, 1940.

Kettl, Donald F. *Deficit Politics: Public Budgeting in its Institutional and Historical Context*. New York: Macmillan, 1992.

Light, Paul C. *The President's Agenda: Domestic Policy Choice from Kennedy to Reagan*. Baltimore, MD: Johns Hopkins University Press, 1991.

Neustadt, Richard E. *Presidential Politics and the Modern Presidents*. New York: Free Press, 1990.

Pfiffner, James P. *The Strategic Presidency: Hitting the Ground Running*. 2nd ed. Lawrence: University Press of Kansas, 1996.

Shull, Steven A. *Domestic Policy Formation: Presidential-Congressional Partnership?* Westport, CT: Greenwood Press, 1983.

Wildavsky, Aaron. *The New Politics of the Budgetary Process*. Medina, OH: Scott, Foresman and Company, 1988.

Chapter 7
Reform, Change, and
Prospects for the Future

The United States and its Constitution are now in their third
century. The passage from each century to the next has been
eventful. The election of 1800 was bitter and personal. The
contest was between two incumbents: John Adams serving as
president, Thomas Jefferson as vice president. Much of the
campaign was carried on in the partisan press. Jefferson won with
seventy-three electoral votes but his running mate, Aaron Burr,
had an equal number of votes. Burr refused to concede and it took
thirty-six ballots in the House of Representatives for Jefferson to
win. As a result, power was transferred from the Federalists to the
Democratic-Republicans. "In demonstrating the young republic's
capacity to effect such a change, the election of 1800 was a
momentous event."[1]

The election at the turn into the twentieth century was a rematch
between the incumbent president, William McKinley, and the
populist William Jennings Bryan. Many of the difficult issues
associated with changes from an agrarian to an industrialized
society were being accommodated, if not resolved. New problems
related to a larger world role for the United States were
developing. McKinley, who hardly campaigned, was reelected
easily but not overwhelmingly. The two-party system continued to
face challenges from third parties, notably the Progressives in the
early years of the new century. With McKinley's death by

assassination in 1901, a dynamic successor, Teddy Roosevelt, shouldered the country into the new century.

The 2000 presidential election joins these other "turn of the century" contests as being historic. Democratic dominance of Congress had been broken six years earlier, and the election of George W. Bush brought the first all-Republican government to Washington in nearly fifty years. Bush's election was among the most contentious in history, showcasing, as it did, sour relations between an impeached President Clinton and the Republican Congress, and the frustrations of Democrats serving in the minority. Having the election settled by the Supreme Court and Bush losing the popular vote added to an intensely partisan mood in the nation's capital.

These three contests also reveal changes in the presidency. The president's constitutional authority has remained essentially the same, but the circumstances under which this authority is exercised are dramatically different at each century's end. The presidency was being formed when Jefferson was inaugurated. It was more a person than an institution, with the incumbent seeking to comprehend the extent and meaning of his powers.

By 1900 the presidency was beginning its ascendancy. *Congressional Government,* as Woodrow Wilson titled his treatise in 1885, could manage the issues of an agrarian society. Industrialization and growth of the world economy required the professionalism of bureaucracy, hierarchy, and executive control, including that by the chief executive. Take-over President Theodore Roosevelt welcomed these responsibilities, as did Woodrow Wilson and Franklin D. Roosevelt. Other presidents of the first third of the century, Taft, Harding, Coolidge, and Hoover, were less moved to embrace an expansive view of presidential power. Still the die was cast. From FDR forward, the presidency would grow in status, influence, and structure.

In two hundred years, the presidency had changed from that of a person—Washington followed by Adams, then Jefferson—to a presidential enterprise with a cast of thousands. Richard E. Neustadt expressed it this way as he reviewed "The President at Mid-Century:" "President and presidency are synonymous no longer; the office now comprises an officialdom."[2] The White House remains the symbolic location of the presidency but it can house only a small portion of those working for the president. Accordingly, George W. Bush's principal task as president-elect in 2000 was to fill jobs, beginning with a personnel director.

This review suggests an important lesson in considering the presidency in the twenty-first century: Events, the issues they generate, and the people who serve are normally more important than reforms in explaining change. Neustadt again: "The presidency nowadays [has] a different look. . . . But . . . that look was not conjured up by statutes, or by staffing. These, rather, are *responses* to the impacts of external circumstances upon our form of government; not causes but effects."[3] This lesson should not come as a surprise. After all, the presidency is a vital institution in a representative democracy. As such it may be expected to respond to events, to include making adjustments so as to function more effectively.

Reform and Change

"Compared with nations elsewhere in the world, Americans have long been among the most enthusiastic reformers."[4] The presidency is a frequent object of reformers. It is thought by many to be the most powerful branch in the separated system. Therefore, it is excessively credited and blamed, depending on the success or failure of government actions. Of the three branches, Congress is most prone to propose reforms because it competes regularly with the presidency for shares of powers. The judiciary's role in this competition is at a greater distance and depends on the circumstance of a case. Court decisions typically set conditions for reforms, then to be designed by others.

What is meant by *reform*? How does it differ from *change*? As used here, reforms are major efforts to alter the structure or authority of the presidency. They refer to those cases where the sole intent is to rearrange how the institution works. New authority to implement policy is not included. For example, the Twenty-second Amendment limiting the president to two terms is most definitely a reform; granting the president the authority to set emission standards to improve air quality is not.

Congress, the competing branch, typically proposes root-and-branch institutional reform of the presidency. It rarely works the other way around: presidential endorsement of congressional reform (and is strongly resented on Capitol Hill if tried). Members of Congress regularly warn that presidential prerogatives can lead to an "imperial presidency" that distorts the separation of equal powers.[5] These worries have led to statutes and constitutional amendments to correct anomalies or impose restraints.

Reforms seldom produce the desired change. They are typically motivated by disagreement with a substantive decision (for example, to go to war). However, the correction tends to be procedural (for example, change *how* decisions to commit troops are made). Unfortunately for the reformer, changing organization, rules, or processes is no guarantee of an acceptable outcome. Reforms typically have unanticipated consequences; changes are those consequences.

The distinction between reform and change is especially well summarized in this statement by Erwin C. Hargrove and Michael Nelson: "Presidential leadership and national politics are inexorably intertwined."[6] What is happening in the nation is, and should be, represented in Washington at both ends of Pennsylvania Avenue. As Hargrove and Nelson document, reformers ordinarily have a preferred model of how presidents should behave. But these "designs by experts" rarely explain the real responses to events and issues that produce changes in governance. Donald F. Kettl wisely attributes response and change to the original design: "The mark of the genius of American founders . . . is in the system's remarkable ability to stretch, change, and adapt—without breaking—as new problems present themselves."[7]

Selected Reforms and Their Effects

Reforms can be made in several manners: constitutional amendments, statutes, court decisions, customs, and expectations. Also varied are the intentions for effecting change: correcting a defect, improving a governmental process, reorganizing government, delegating authority, clarifying or limiting authority, reallocating powers, and expanding prerogatives. Reform is sometimes motivated by a judgment that power holders have gone too far in the exercise of their authority and at other times because authority has not been used previously to suit a particular situation. Both urges have been illustrated since 9/11 as a consequence of coping with an unfamiliar war on terrorism. As Kettl argues, reformers often aim to make the executive more accountable. But measuring accountability for what happens in a system of divided authority is difficult, yet essential if reform is to be effective.[8] Put otherwise, separating powers diffuses accountability, thus making it challenging in the extreme to centralize it without rearranging the constitutional order.

Constitutional Amendments

Given the complexity of the amending process (requiring super majorities at both the congressional and state levels), one does not expect it to happen often. There are nine amendments directly affecting the presidency. They are of three types: corrections to omissions or anomalies in the original document, expansions of the voting franchise, and limiting terms.

As shown in table 7.1, the Twelfth, Twentieth, Twenty-third, and Twenty-fifth Amendments provided needed corrections to the Constitution. The amendments had varying effects. The Twelfth was vital, as has been discussed previously. The Twentieth and

Table 7.1 Reforms as Constitutional Amendments

Type 1: Correction

Amendment (ratified)	Purpose
Twelfth (1804)	Electors vote separately for president and vice president
Twentieth (1933)	Presidential term ends January 20 rather than March 4 (set by Congress in 1792)
Twenty-third (1961)	District of Columbia provided with three electoral votes
Twenty-fifth (1967)	Fill a vice-presidential vacancy and provide method for managing when the president is unable to discharge duties

Type 2: Expand Voting Franchise

Fifteenth (1870)	Right to vote extended to African Americans
Nineteenth (1920)	Right extended to women
Twenty-fourth (1964)	Right cannot be denied for failure to pay a poll tax
Twenty-sixth (1971)	Age eligibility lowered to 18

Type 3: Two-Term Limitation

Twenty-second (1951)	Presidents limited to two terms

Source: Compiled by the author.

Twenty-fifth also had important and desirable effects. Imagine today having the new president take office on March 4, four months after the election, rather than January 20. Remarkably this change in the Twentieth Amendment was not made until 1933.

Vice presidents have come to play important roles in recent presidencies, certainly from Carter forward. The provision for replacing the vice president has been used twice since its inception—Gerald Ford when Spiro Agnew resigned in 1973 and Nelson Rockefeller when Ford became president following Nixon's resignation, August 9, 1974. The provision also would have been invoked in 1999 had Clinton been removed by the Senate following his impeachment in the House in 1998. Replacement President Gore would have nominated a vice president to serve with him, 1999–2001.

Had Nixon been impeached and removed from office in 1974 (as was threatened by some Democrats prior to Nixon's resignation), there would have been no vice president to take over had the Twenty-fifth Amendment not been passed and ratified. Under those conditions, the Speaker of the House, Carl Albert, a Democrat from Oklahoma, would have assumed the presidency, a prospect he did not welcome.

The Fifteenth, Nineteenth, and Twenty-sixth Amendments attuned suffrage to contemporary trends—assuring African Americans and women the right to vote and lowering the eligible age to eighteen. The Twenty-fourth Amendment was a long overdue guarantee of the right to vote free of having to pay a poll tax. The suffrage amendments would, over time, transform the nature of presidential campaigns. Each resulted in huge increases in the number of eligible voters. It took time, however, for turnout among these voters to increase.

The one remaining amendment, the Twenty-second, revisited a debate thought to have been settled at the Constitutional

Convention. Presidents by custom had limited themselves to two terms. FDR did not. With the end of World War II and the extraordinary executive powers of a president reelected three times, a two-term limitation amendment was introduced soon after the Republican Congress met in 1947. It quickly passed both houses by the required two-thirds majorities and was sent to the states for ratification, which occurred four years later. Historian Forrest McDonald dubbed it "a posthumous slap at Roosevelt."[9]

The effect of the Twenty-second Amendment is uncertain. It first applied to Eisenhower (as the incumbent at the time the amendment was proposed, Truman was excluded from the limitation). Judging the effect requires evaluating an imponderable: Would those serving two full terms seek a third? Age and health likely would have led Eisenhower and Reagan to pass on a third term. That leaves Clinton (Bush 43 still serving a second term at this writing). Age in Clinton's case may have weighed in favor of his seeking a third term. He was fifty-four at the end of his second term.

What can be said is that the amendment has replaced a question mark with a period. Will the president seek a third term? He cannot. As a consequence, the election following a reelection (for example, 1960, 1988, 2000, and potentially 2008) will feature open races in both parties. As a consequence, a presidential campaign may be expected to begin soon after the inauguration of the second-term president. Many of the candidates are likely to be serving on Capitol Hill, mostly in the Senate, anxious to augment their records in anticipation of the campaign. Meanwhile, the president's cabinet and staff know their time too is limited, thus encouraging thoughts about their careers. Overcoming this rush to the future so as to manage the present is a major challenge for a term-limited leader, one of those unanticipated consequences of reform.

Statutes

Most reforms and adaptations to change occur through the ordinary lawmaking process. Regular work on Capitol Hill and in the White House is less consciously reformist than simply trying to discover the best or most feasible way to manage the agenda. For example, when programs like Medicare and Medicaid are put in place over a period of years, Congress authorizes the executive to do what is necessary organizationally and procedurally for effective implementation. One consequence of the passage of such massive programs is a significant expansion of the bureaucracy and increased presidential responsibilities. Reform was intended in these cases but directed to health care delivery, not institutional growth.

Members of Congress are charged with overseeing the administration of such programs, but in reality they are dependent on the executive, even in the exercise of oversight. That dependency is one measure of the power of the executive in relationship to the legislature.

It is worth noting that presidents do not always welcome these greater responsibilities. In fact, those presidents inheriting entitlement programs may seek to curb their growth because of the effect of uncontrollable spending on the deficit, which, in turn, limits presidential options for inaugurating new programs.

In addition to legislation on substantive policy matters (for example, agriculture, welfare, health care, crime) laws are passed from time to time that are designed to bolster or constrain presidential prerogatives or affect how they do their politics. Such laws are ordinarily more directly reformist in intent. Those designing such legislation want to change the "how" and "who" of decision making, not just the "what." Table 7.2 provides a sample of such laws for the twentieth and into the twenty-first centuries. These fifteen laws represent efforts to reform the presidency and the executive branch in regard to six vital functions: budgeting, the

Table 7.2 Reforms as Statutes: Selected Cases

Legislation	Reform
Budgeting	
Budget and Accounting Act of 1921	Created first national budget system, established the Bureau of the Budget (BOB)
Congressional Budget and Impoundment, Control Act of 1974	Designed congressional budget, established Congressional Budget Office (CBO) and limited president's authority to impound funds
Gramm-Rudman-Hollings Anti-Deficit Act of 1985	Established automatic spending adjustments with a goal of balancing the budget
Line-item veto of 1996	Authorized a process for president to veto specific projects. Declared unconstitutional by the Supreme Court
The Economy	
Federal Reserve Act of 1913	Established an independent system for monetary policy, with a Board of Governors
Reciprocal Trade Agreement Act of 1934	Authorized president to enter into commercial trade agreements with foreign nations
Employment Act of 1946	Created president's Council of Economic Advisers (CEA) and provided for reports on the state of the economy
Reorganization	
Reorganization Plan of 1939 (and subsequent plans)	Created Executive Office of the President (EOP), moved BOB to EOP (from Treasury), increased presidential staff. Followed by other plans expanding EOP

(*continued*)

Table 7.2 (*continued*)

Legislation	Reform
National Security	
National Security Act of 1947	Reorganized military service into a Department of Defense, created National Security Council (NSC) and staff in EOP, also the Central Intelligence Agency (CIA)
War Powers Act of 1973	Limited president's authority to commit troops to combat. Set timetables for reports and withdrawal when declaration of war lacking. Passed over Nixon's veto
National Commission on Terrorist Attacks, 2002	Authorized appointment of commission to explore intelligence failures prior to 9/11 and to make recommendations
Intelligence Overhaul of 2004	Reorganization of intelligence agencies, authorizing appointment of a director to coordinate intelligence services, including the CIA
Campaigning	
Federal Election Campaign Act of 1974	Provided public funding of presidential campaigns, created Federal Election Commission (FEC)
Bipartisan Campaign Reform Act of 2002	Restrictions on raising soft money and other limits on financing campaigns
Public Access	
Freedom of Information Act Amendments of 1974	Major expansion of the 1966 act providing public access to government documents. Enacted over Ford's veto

Source: Compiled by author from various sources.

economy, organizational capacity, national security, campaigning, and public access. Most of the laws aim to strengthen or restrict the presidency; some are designed to strengthen Congress so it may compete more effectively with the executive branch.

It is apparent in reviewing these laws that the overall trend is toward a greater role for the president, interspersed by efforts to check or control that growth. Most of the developments followed logically from the growth and complexity of government programs. Budgeting came to be increasingly important, requiring the expertise of economic and accounting specialists. And so that function was concentrated in the executive. Congress became anxious because of its dependency on the executive and formed its own process in 1974, which included hiring its own budget specialists.

Similar trends are noted in regard to the economy, national security policy, and the institutionalization of the presidency. Presidents are commonly held responsible for the state of the economy, even as they have limited tools for managing it. Thus, for example, the independent Federal Reserve Board has substantially more authority to influence economic developments by its role in monetary policy. Congress has authorized support for economic management, and presidents have reorganized within the White House for this purpose (the formation of a National Economic Council in 1993 by executive order being one such recent change).

The president's role in national security policy has a constitutional basis, given the status of commander in chief. That position was substantially formalized with the organizational unity of the military services and the creation of a National Security Council and staff in 1947. As with budgeting, Congress has from time to time expressed concern about the president's dominance, thus the efforts to limit military engagements without a declaration of war by Congress or to investigate national security decision making when things go wrong. These actions are not without effect, but the president continues to lead when it comes to foreign and national security policy.

The presidency continues to grow as an institution. The critical point came in 1939 with the creation of the Executive Office of the President (EOP). The name itself acknowledged the need for an umbrella organization to shelter the many advisory units required to match the growth of government programs. And so with each extension—national security, the economy, the environment, trade, science—another "office" or "council" joined the all-important Office of Management and Budget in the EOP. Taken together with the White House Office, these are the units that form the presidential branch discussed earlier.

I have also included two other types of statutes—campaigning and public access. The first is most often a story of frustration for reformers. Attention is paid primarily to campaign finance, the concern being the amount of money spent and its sources. New laws change how money is raised, but they have not curbed the amounts and have had variable effects on who gives. Finally, the Freedom of Information Act, as amended, has benefited the media and scholars while encouraging caution within the executive branch about producing and preserving documents.

These statutes illustrate the intricate politics of reform in a separated powers government. Ever attentive to institutional status, the branches protect their prerogatives and often resent those of others. Accordingly, designs for change in response to events and agenda shifts are scrutinized carefully at both ends of Pennsylvania Avenue for how they affect the balance of powers.

What are the effects and lessons of statutory reform? First, it is apparent that representative government will respond to what goes on outside the capital. It is logical, for example, for executives to prepare budgets and manage the military. And that is what has occurred, even though it reduces the influence of the representative legislature. Second, logic has dictated the expansion of the executive during the twentieth and into the twenty-first centuries. Many of the statutes cited previously have resulted in greater responsibilities for presidents (if not necessarily greater powers)—regarding the budget, military, war making, economy, and social life. Third, just as evident is the failure of Congress to keep pace. Members have tried by creating a budget process, reorganizing committees, expanding staff, adding legislative agencies, and demanding more executive accountability. But the challenges are immense of preparing legislation and overseeing its implementation. Fourth, it is well-nigh impossible to turn back the clock. I have included the War Powers Act primarily to illustrate that fact. War has been in the process of redefinition for decades. The most recent iteration—the war on terrorism—has stimulated further debate and puzzlement regarding the sharing of powers among the branches.

Supreme Court Decisions

The third source of reform and change of the presidency is the Supreme Court. Supreme Court justices are not reformers by the nature of their jobs. Whatever their personal beliefs, their place of work does not foster taking such initiatives. Yet their decisions can have the effect of enhancing, clarifying, or thwarting authority as exercised by the president. It is generally accepted that the Supreme Court will uphold executive powers. After all, not to do so is a case of one branch overruling another. Those occasions when they happen are, therefore, attention getting.

At least three types of decisions can have an effect on presidential power. First are decisions that strike down law favored by the president as exceeding his authority. For example, President Franklin D. Roosevelt proposed bold legislation to deal with the Great Depression. Several programs were struck down by the Supreme Court, notably a proposal in the National Industrial Recovery Act to set industry codes of fair competition (*Schechter Poultry Corporation v. United States*, 1935) and provisions of the Agriculture Adjustment Act (*United States v. Butler*, 1936).

Second are decisions regarding legislation proposed by others. The Federal Election Campaign Act Amendments of 1974 were proposed and passed during the Watergate scandals. Among their many provisions, the Amendments set contribution and spending limits. The Supreme Court declared the latter in violation of the First Amendment right of free speech (*Buckley v. Valeo*, 1976). That ruling meant that campaign expenditures would continue to escalate, making it imperative that presidential candidates have access to huge sums of money.

Third are those decisions it is said the Supreme Court wishes to avoid: those striking down uses of executive authority. Table 7.3 shows selected cases. The decisions illustrate the circumstantial nature of Supreme Court involvement. Put otherwise, it is difficult to generalize about these decisions for predicting future decisions, apart from the Supreme Court's attention to presidential overreaching in dealing with unprecedented situations.

Removals of those appointed were the subjects of the *Myers* and *Humphries* cases. Clarification was essential as new agencies and appointing procedures were instituted. *Myers* allowed removal of those appointed with Senate concurrence; *Humphries* restricted removal of those in a growing number of independent regulatory commissions.

Two cases involved unprecedented wartime situations. President Truman was concerned during the Korean War that a pending strike against the steel industry would harm the production of needed war material. He ordered the seizure of the mills, presumably relying on his powers as commander in chief. The Court rejected Truman's interpretation of his authority. Much later, President George W. Bush faced the exceptional circumstance of trying alleged or suspected terrorists with no common national identity. His solution was to establish separate military tribunals, done without requesting congressional approval. Again the Court rejected his interpretation of

Table 7.3 Interpreting Presidential Power: Selected Supreme Court Cases

Case	Decision
Myers v. United States (1926)	President does not need Senate approval to remove those appointed with Senate approval
Humphries Executor v. United States (1935)	Limited the president's power to remove members of independent regulatory commissions
Youngstown Sheet & Tube Co. v. Sawyer (1952)	Declared President Truman's seizure of steel mills during the Korean War as an unconstitutional act
United States v. Nixon (1974)	Rejected President Nixon's claim of executive privilege in refusing to turn over Oval Office tapes to the special prosecutor
Clinton v. Jones (1997)	Incumbent president is not protected by the Constitution from civil litigation; suit by Paula Jones can go forward
Clinton et al. v. New York City et al. (1998)	Line-item veto provided to president by Congress is unconstitutional
Bush v. Gore (2000)	Recount procedures designated by the Florida Supreme Court were unconstitutional (holding applied to the present case)
Hamdan v. Rumsfeld (2006)	Military commissions established by President Bush to try suspected terrorists are unconstitutional

Source: Compiled by the author from various sources.

presidential authority, while inviting Congress to act (*Hamdan v. Rumsfeld*), and it did late in the 109th Congress by providing for military commissions to prosecute terrorism suspects.

United States v. Nixon and *Clinton v. Jones* were special as cases in which the president sought to prevent potentially damaging evidence from entering the judicial process. Nixon invoked executive privilege to prevent tapes of Oval Office conversations from being used by the Watergate special prosecutor. The Court rejected his claim, which eventually led to Nixon's resignation. Clinton wished to prevent a civil action by Paula Jones from going forward while he was still in office. The Court decided that such an action would not interfere with the exercise of presidential duties. Both cases were unanimously decided against the president.

The other two cases in table 7.3 have little in common. A Republican Congress provided for a line-item veto during Clinton's presidency, authority he asked for, as had presidents before him. The Court could find no constitutional basis for such an action. And the Court decided in 2000 to halt the Florida recount and, for all practical purposes, award the presidency to George W. Bush. Sensitive to the extraordinary circumstance of resolving an election dispute, the Court emphasized that its decision applied only to the present case.

Court decisions regarding the presidency are not reforms as much as clarifications with implications for change. When Congress and the president make adaptations to suit new or developing circumstances, the Court may accept a case asking it to judge whether such actions meet constitutional muster. *Marbury v. Madison* (1803) is cited in some of these cases: "It is emphatically the province and duty of the judicial department to say what the law is." Thus, for example, if a president claims he has executive privilege or that a decision is in accordance with inherent powers, the Court may hear a challenge and decide whether or not the president is correct.

Perhaps the broadest lesson for presidents from this review is this: When in doubt, rely on the separation of powers. Primarily that message suggests getting congressional approval or judicial clearance (at minimum by carefully examining court precedents). It advises against going it alone except in crises where time is of the essence. A related lesson is that presidents should be cautious about asserting powers to protect them against charges regarding their personal behavior. When this happens, presidents are saying what the law is rather than are the courts.

Customs and Expectations

Changes in customs and what the public and others expect of the presidency also have effects. These features are more amorphous than those discussed above, yet no less indicative of governmental, political, and societal developments.

Fig. 7.1. President Roosevelt's Joint Press Conference with Prime Minister Churchill on December 23, 1941 (AP Images)

Customs are ordinary ways of doing things, as with habits or routines. New circumstances typically establish new customs. For example, FDR met twice a week with reporters in the Oval Office. They crowded around his desk to ask questions. His responses were ordinarily off the record. Apart from major addresses, Roosevelt's communication with the public was also low key. He inaugurated fireside chats on the radio, "a revolutionary advance in the presidential use of the mass media" when first tried.[10]

The transformation in communications and travel dramatically changed how presidents and their staffs now interact with the press and public. Meetings with reporters are not only on the record for the press but are typically viewed as well by anyone who has an interest. Transcripts are available on websites. Presidents travel with greater frequency than ever, campaigning for public support of their program. President Clinton went on the road immediately after delivering the State of the Union message to justify and defend his proposals, a practice that has come to be "customary" for his successor, George W. Bush.

Customary roles of those in the White House entourage have changed markedly. In the past, First Ladies were seldom judged to be public figures in their own right (Eleanor Roosevelt being a major exception). Not anymore. Hillary Clinton was put in charge of a national health care proposal. Vice presidents had few functions, little staff, and no official residence. State of the Union messages were sent to Congress, not delivered. And security at the White House was lax. All of that, and more, has changed.

These developments have also contributed to altered expectations of the president and the presidency. Expectations may be in two forms. First are those associated with what the press and public come to know about the person—background, philosophy, values. Second are the anticipations related to the presidency—notably its leadership role in the separated system and its status in the world.

These two images are not always in harmony and can change during time in office.

A few examples illustrate: Truman had to deal with incongruous expectations—low for him due to his lack of executive experience; high for the presidency following the three plus terms of FDR. Eisenhower's background as a military leader was expected to restore the image of the presidency following Truman. Watergate and its aftermath (to include President Ford's pardoning of Nixon) had a negative effect on the image of the presidency, thus creating a major challenge for Carter, a president with no Washington experience. Bush 41 was among the most qualified presidents by the measure of executive experience, but his presidency was shaped by expectations born of the leadership of his predecessor, Ronald Reagan. And Bush 43 was confronted with a presidency diminished by his predecessor's impeachment and resulting partisan conflict, yet one facing questions about the new president's competence and the legitimacy of his victory.

Meanwhile, growing demands for presidential leadership are accompanied by expectations of greater accountability. The expansion of federal government programs and the interconnectedness among nations that is globalization help to explain why most eyes are directed to Washington and the White House.

Looking Ahead: The New Realities

The future of the presidency is heavily influenced by its past and present. The most reliable way to look ahead is through the prism of current politics. The constitutional status of the presidency has undergone relatively few changes. The most important of these occurred more than fifty years ago—a two-term limitation. Apart from the quadrennial proposals to reform the Electoral College, no serious amendments to Article II are contemplated. And so the core function—"The executive power shall be vested in a President of the United States of America"—remains the same.

What has changed is the context within which executive power is exercised. That is true through history, as I have sought to illustrate. What in the present setting aids in predicting the future? The political, policy, and administrative landscapes are notably relevant in assessing presidential power in this new century.

Political

Little or nothing in the political landscape suggests change in the narrow margins that have been featured since 1992. The shift from a strongly Democratic South to Republican dominance in that region has solidified an intensely competitive two-party system. The tight split is popularized by a red state/blue state map and referred to with a shorthand phrase: polarization. Much of the analysis has a reformist tinge in suggesting that the split is a condition to be corrected. Meanwhile, the reality is that presidential and congressional elections are likely to be closely decided and not that subject to manipulation on a national scale.

Narrow margins can easily result in split-party government. One senator leaving his party for independent status in 2001 shifted Senate majority control from the Republicans to the Democrats. Changes in a few votes in Florida in 2000 and Ohio in 2004 and the Democrats would have won the White House, very likely both times with a Republican Congress. The 2006 mid-term elections resulted in a 49–49 tie in the Senate, with two Independents voting with the Democrats to organize the chamber.

These realities have had a profound effect on the presidency. The incentives are competitive and partisan, not cooperative and bipartisan. Presidents have to design strategies that acknowledge small margins, partisanship, and intense competition, yet be prepared to compromise at key junctures in the lawmaking process. A premium may also be placed on confidentiality, even concealment, of plans and decisions. Presidents in narrow-margin politics are likely also to be attentive to the importance of party discipline in Congress, taking care not to undermine House and Senate leadership efforts by entering into cross-party agreements in the early stages of lawmaking.

The partisan incentives of narrow margins and split control are likely to be pervasive, with a potent minority exercising every available tactic to force compromise. The more the minority obstructs, the more the majority seeks additional partisan advantages, particularly in the House of Representatives. Often these conditions result in a reduced role for the president, who becomes an observer more than a participant.

However unappealing, this landscape need not be perilous to lawmaking. As has been shown, laws do get enacted, crises overcome partisanship, and both parties, not just the governing party, have incentives to participate actively in policy making. The point is that the context for exercising presidential power is different. It is also perfectly legitimate in a system of separated powers, a detail sometimes lost in a fervor for reform.

Policy

Subject as it is to events, the policy agenda is ever changing. Predictions are therefore somewhat less supportable than with the other landscapes. For example, what had settled into a primarily domestic set of issues during the Clinton presidency and into the early months of the Bush 43 first term was dramatically altered by 9/11. That event spawned issues that appear to "have legs," as the phrase has it. Accordingly, it is likely that presidents in the near term will face the policy uncertainties of unfamiliar wars.

Perhaps foremost of these sureties is the effect of national security on the rest of the agenda. Terrorism has had an acute effect as a dominant issue in and of itself, and for its influence on how other issues are defined. For itself, combating terrorism involves a stateless war, one in which the enemy may be concealed within several countries, including the United States. For its effect otherwise, issues such as immigration, port security, international trade and finance, federal-state-local policing functions, to name a few, are profoundly affected.

An issue of such wide-ranging proportions will elicit serious debate and criticism. The adage from earlier times that such debate should stop at the water's edge, preferably with bipartisan support for the president, no longer holds. Almost by definition, rules based on what is known (for example, conventional war) are difficult to apply to the unfamiliar (for example, a stateless war on terrorism). Future presidents cannot expect national security and foreign policy decisions to receive automatic approval by Congress, the media, or the public, possibly apart from a catastrophe akin to that on 9/11.

As noted, the war on terrorism, American military and political engagements in the Middle East, and the development of nuclear weapons capabilities in unfriendly regimes have influenced how domestic issues are interpreted. Yet there are other realities associated with homeland issues. Most such matters derive from programs already on the books. "Reform" is incorporated into nearly all major presidential proposals: Social Security reform, Medicare reform, immigration reform, environmental reform. The domestic agenda is primarily generated from what the government is already doing. That fact is unlikely to change with a new administration. Presidents in 2008, 2012, 2016, and for as long as the eyes can see will find it difficult to initiate new programs or kill existing programs so as to find a place for something new.

Administrative

The costs of entitlements and military preparedness have increased exponentially with limited or no controls. Spending has become automatic. Formulas and events determine expenditures with revenues failing to keep pace and narrow-margin politics making it difficult to hike taxes. Deficits result and the public debt increases. An effort was made by President Clinton and a Republican Congress to balance future budgets in 1997, but events and politics prevailed to set record deficits and debt after 2001.

A famous western song is titled "Don't Fence Me In." It is no exaggeration to imagine presidential power as "fenced in." Presidents are managers of debt. Promises are made during campaigns but are kept only when the president can find a revenue-neutral means for implementing them or is convincing enough so that the need is more important than adding to the debt.

Less noticed as an administrative development is the federalization of government programs. Presidents and their appointees administer much of the domestic agenda through two, three, or more layers of government. Adaptations may be permitted to allow for regional, state, or local circumstances. This process has now been extended to homeland security.

Small wonder that the presidency has developed its own branch of specialists. Presidents want and need assistants who will guide them through the pathways of program development, enactment, and delivery. It has been typical for succeeding presidents to retain positions created by their predecessors. The White House has long since ceased to be merely the Executive Mansion. It is now that branch of government struggling to manage that for which presidents will be held accountable.

Conclusion

The American presidency is not the American government. It is, rather, a leadership contrivance for managing the executive branch, working interactively with the legislative and judicial branches. The presidency has changed, adapting to national and international developments. And it has been reformed, most notably by imposing a two-term limitation. Even at this writing, however, the place to start in understanding the presidency is the separation-of-powers scheme as set forth in the Constitution. For it is in that document that the president, members of Congress, and judges were to be separately chosen to serve assorted term lengths. Independently selected, these officials make, administer, and evaluate law interdependently.

The lesson is clear. Effective presidential power in a separated system is that exercised in recognition of the legitimate functions of the other branches. E. Pendleton Herring described the presidency so well: "We have created a position of great power but have made the full realization of that power dependent upon influence rather than legal authority."[11] Accordingly, study of the presidency should acknowledge the president's political status and style within the constitutional structure. That has been the emphasis in these pages.

Notes

1. Noble E. Cunningham, Jr., *In Pursuit of Reason: The Life of Thomas Jefferson* (Baton Rouge: Louisiana State University Press, 1987), 237. The Twelfth Amendment later corrected the fault; see chapter 3.
2. Richard E. Neustadt, "The Presidency at Mid-Century," *Law and Contemporary Politics* 21 (Autumn 1956): 609–45.
3. Ibid. Emphasis in original.
4. Donald F. Kettl, "Reforming the Executive Branch of the U. S. Government," in *The Executive Branch*, ed. Joel D. Aberbach and Mark A. Peterson (New York: Oxford University Press, 2005), 344.
5. Their case is set forth in an influential book written by Arthur M. Schlesinger, Jr., during the Nixon presidency: *The Imperial Presidency* (New York: Houghton Mifflin, 1973). Schlesinger worried most about the president's powers in foreign and national security policy, where a "runaway presidency" could lead to excessive power at home, vii–x.

6. Erwin C. Hargrove and Michael Nelson, *Presidents, Politics, and Policy* (Baltimore, MD: Johns Hopkins University Press, 1984), 271.
7. Kettl, "Reforming," 344.
8. Ibid., 369–70.
9. Forrest McDonald, *The American Presidency: An Intellectual History* (Lawrence: University Press of Kansas, 1994), 407.
10. Michael Nelson, ed., *Congressional Quarterly's Guide to the Presidency,* 2nd ed. (Washington, DC: Congressional Quarterly Press, 1996), 124.
11. E. Pendleton Herring, *Presidential Leadership* (New York: Rinehart and Company, 1940), 2–3.

References

Aberbach, Joel D., and Mark A. Peterson, eds. *The Executive Branch.* New York: Oxford University Press, 2005.

Hargrove, Erwin C. *The President as Leader.* Lawrence: University Press of Kansas, 1998.

Herring, E. Pendleton. *Presidential Leadership.* New York: Rinehart and Company, 1940.

Nelson, Michael, ed. *Congressional Quarterly's Guide to the Presidency.* 2nd ed. Washington, DC: Congressional Quarterly Press, 1996.

Neustadt, Richard E. *Presidential Power: The Politics of Leadership.* New York: John Wiley, 1960.

Appendix

Presidents and Vice Presidents of the United States of America, 1789–2009

Year	President	Vice President	Party	Vote %
1789	Washington	Adams	Federalist	EV=100*
1792	Washington	Adams	Federalist	EV=98
1796	Adams	Jefferson	Federalist/ Democratic Republican**	EV=51
1800	Jefferson	Burr	Democratic Republican	EV=53***
1804	Jefferson	G. Clinton	Democratic Republican	EV=92
1808	Madison	G. Clinton	Democratic Republican	EV=69
1812	Madison	Gerry	Democratic Republican	EV=59
1816	Monroe	Tompkins	Democratic Republican	EV=83

(continued)

Year	President	Vice President	Party	Vote %
1820	Monroe	Tompkins	Democratic Republican	EV = 98
1824	J. Q. Adams	Calhoun	Democratic Republican	PV = 31 EV = 32***
1828	Jackson	Calhoun	Democratic Republican	PV = 56 EV = 68
1832	Jackson	Van Buren	Democrat	PV = 54 EV = 76
1836	Van Buren	R. Johnson	Democrat	PV = 51 EV = 58
1840	W. Harrison	Tyler#	Whig	PV = 53 EV = 80
1844	Polk	Dallas	Democrat	PV = 50 EV = 62
1848	Taylor	Fillmore#	Whig	PV = 47 EV = 56
1852	Pierce	King	Democrat	PV = 51 EV = 86
1856	Buchanan	Breckinridge	Democrat	PV = 45 EV = 59
1860	Lincoln	Hamlin	Republican	PV = 40 EV = 59
1864	Lincoln	A. Johnson#	Republican	PV = 55 EV = 91
1868	Grant	Colfax	Republican	PV = 53 EV = 73
1872	Grant	H. Wilson	Republican	PV = 56 EV = 78

(*continued*)

Year	President	Vice President	Party	Vote %
1876	Hayes	Wheeler	Republican	PV = 48 EV = 50+
1880	Garfield	Arthur#	Republican	PV = 48 EV = 58
1884	Cleveland	Hendricks	Democrat	PV = 49 EV = 55
1888	B. Harrison	Morton	Republican	PV = 48 EV = 58
1892	Cleveland	Stevenson	Democrat	PV = 46 EV = 62
1896	McKinley	Hobart	Republican	PV = 51 EV = 61
1900	McKinley	T. Roosevelt#	Republican	PV = 52 EV = 65
1904	T. Roosevelt	Fairbanks	Republican	PV = 56 EV – 71
1908	Taft	Sherman	Republican	PV = 52 EV = 66
1912	W. Wilson	Marshall	Democrat	PV = 42 EV = 82
1916	Wilson	Marshall	Democrat	PV = 49 EV = 52
1920	Harding	Coolidge#	Republican	PV = 60 EV = 76
1924	Coolidge	Dawes	Republican	PV = 54 EV = 72
1928	Hoover	Curtis	Republican	PV = 58 EV = 84

(continued)

Year	President	Vice President	Party	Vote %
1932	F. Roosevelt	Garner	Democrat	PV = 57 EV = 89
1936	F. Roosevelt	Garner	Democrat	PV = 61 EV = 98
1940	F. Roosevelt	Wallace	Democrat	PV = 55 EV = 85
1944	F. Roosevelt	Truman#	Democrat	PV = 53 EV = 81
1948	Truman	Barkley	Democrat	PV = 50 EV = 57
1952	Eisenhower	Nixon	Republican	PV = 55 EV = 83
1956	Eisenhower	Nixon	Republican	PV = 57 EV = 86
1960	Kennedy	L. Johnson#	Democrat	PV = 50 EV = 56
1964	L. Johnson	Humphrey	Democrat	PV = 61 EV = 90
1968	Nixon	Agnew	Republican	PV = 43 EV = 56
1972	Nixon	Agnew/ Ford##	Republican	PV = 61 EV = 97
1976	Carter	Mondale	Democrat	PV = 50 EV = 55
1980	Reagan	GHW Bush	Republican	PV = 51 EV = 91
1984	Reagan	GHW Bush	Republican	PV = 59 EV = 98

(*continued*)

Year	President	Vice President	Party	Vote %
1988	GHW Bush	Quayle	Republican	PV = 53 EV = 79
1992	W. Clinton	Gore	Democrat	PV = 43 EV = 69
1996	W. Clinton	Gore	Democrat	PV = 49 EV = 70
2000	GW Bush	Cheney	Republican	PV = 48 EV = 50+
2004	GW Bush	Cheney	Republican	PV = 51 EV = 53

KEY: PV = Popular vote percentage; EV = Electoral vote percentage.

*Popular vote tabulations were not provided until 1824; electoral vote percentage is for the president only; those running second were vice presidents and received a different percentage until the ratification of the Twelfth Amendment.

**Jefferson, running second and serving as vice president, had a different party affiliation.

***Election went to the House of Representatives.

#A takeover president due to the death of the president.

##Agnew resigned as vice president, Ford was appointed under the procedures of the Twenty-second Amendment, then took over when Nixon resigned.

Source: Compiled from data in Michael Nelson, ed., *Congressional Quarterly's Guide to the Presidency* (Congressional Quarterly, 1996), 1667–69.

Index

Index